# Visual Basic

# CD TUTOR

**Clint Hicks**

que

## Visual Basic CD Tutor

**Copyright© 1995 by Que® Corporation.**

Library of Congress Catalog No.: 95-67836

ISBN: 0-7989-0098-0

97  96  95    6  5  4  3  2  1

Interpretation of the printing code: the rightmost double-digit number is the year of the book's printing; the rightmost single-digit number, the number of the book's printing. For example, a printing code of 95-1 shows that the first printing of the book occurred in 1995.

Screen reproductions in this book were created with Collage Plus from Inner Media, Inc., Hollis, NH.

Multimedia presentations were created with Lotus ScreenCam from Lotus Development Corp., Cambridge, MA.

**Publisher:** Roland Elgey

**Associate Publisher:** Joseph P. Wikert

**Director of Product Series:** Charles O. Stewart III

**Managing Editor:** Kelli Widdifield

**Director of Marketing:** Lynn E. Zingraf

# Dedication

*For Allen*

*Best Friend and Best Man*

*1960-1994*

# Credits

**Acquisitions Editor**
Fred Slone

**Product Director**
C. Kazim Haidri

**Production Editor**
Susan Ross Moore

**Copy Editors**
Patrick Kanouse
Theresa Mathias
Nancy E. Sixsmith

**Technical Editors**
Red Deupree
Gary King

**Acquisitions Coordinator**
Angela C. Kozlowski

**Operations Coordinator**
Patricia J. Brooks

**Editorial Assistant**
Michelle R. Williams

**Book Designer**
Sandra Schroeder

**Cover Designers**
Dan Armstrong
Karen Ruggles

**Production Team**
Angela D. Bannan
Claudia Bell
Amy Cornwell
Maxine Dillingham
Chad Dressler
Karen Gregor
Dennis Clay Hager
George Hanlin
Aren Howell
John Hulse
Barry Jorden
Elizabeth Lewis
Erika Millen
Kim Mitchell
Linda Quigley
Kaylene Riemen
Bobbi Satterfield
Kris Simmons
Michael Thomas
Marcella Thompson

**Indexer**
Kathy Venable

Composed in *Stone Serif* and *MCPdigital* by Que Corporation.

# About the Author

**Clint Hicks** has been writing about computers and computer software since 1984. A 1982 graduate of Rice University in Houston, Texas, Clint worked as a technical writer in a number of engineering and software development firms. In 1988 he joined the staff at Peter Norton Computing, Inc. (PNCI). In 1989 he become Manager of Technical Publications; later, he was promoted to Senior Editor. In this capacity he oversaw all aspects of software documentation at PNCI, including writing, editing, layout, and production. Clint has been working as a freelance technical author and editor since 1990.

Clint's specialties include operating systems, utilities, and programming languages. His software documentation and trade computer publications on these subjects have consistently won high praise. The Society for Technical Communication singled out in particular his manual for Version 1.0 of the Norton Utilities for the Macintosh. More recently, his work on MS-DOS was favorably recommended in *The New York Times*.

Currently, Clint lives with his wife, daughter, and son in Santa Fe, New Mexico. Outside interests include physics and astronomy, cooking, gardening, and anthropology; he's currently at work on an advanced degree in the latter subject, focusing on the history of technology in general and the culture of computers in particular.

# Trademark Acknowledgments

All terms mentioned in this book that are known to be trademarks or service marks have been appropriately capitalized. Que Corporation cannot attest to the accuracy of this information. Use of a term in this book should not be regarded as affecting the validity of any trademark or service mark.

# We'd Like to Hear from You!

As part of our continuing effort to produce books of the highest possible quality, Que would like to hear your comments. To stay competitive, we *really* want you, as a computer book reader and user, to let us know what you like or dislike most about this book or other Que products.

You can mail comments, ideas, or suggestions for improving future editions to the address below, or send us a fax at (317) 581-4663. For the on-line inclined, Macmillan Computer Publishing has a forum on CompuServe (type **GO QUEBOOKS** at any prompt) through which our staff and authors are available for questions and comments. The address of our Internet site is **http://www.mcp.com** (World Wide Web).

In addition to exploring our forum, please feel free to contact me personally to discuss your opinions of this book: on CompuServe, I'm at 74143,1574, and on the Internet, I'm **chaidri@que.mcp.com**.

Thanks in advance—your comments will help us to continue publishing the best books available on computer topics in today's market.

Chris Haidri
Product Development Specialist
Que Corporation
201 W. 103rd Street
Indianapolis, Indiana 46290
USA

# Contents at a Glance

# Contents

# II Intermediate Topics                                            109

## 9 Making Decisions                                              111

## 10 Implementing and Editing Menus                              127

## 17 Storing, Retrieving, and Printing Data     227

## 18 Communicating with Other Programs     239

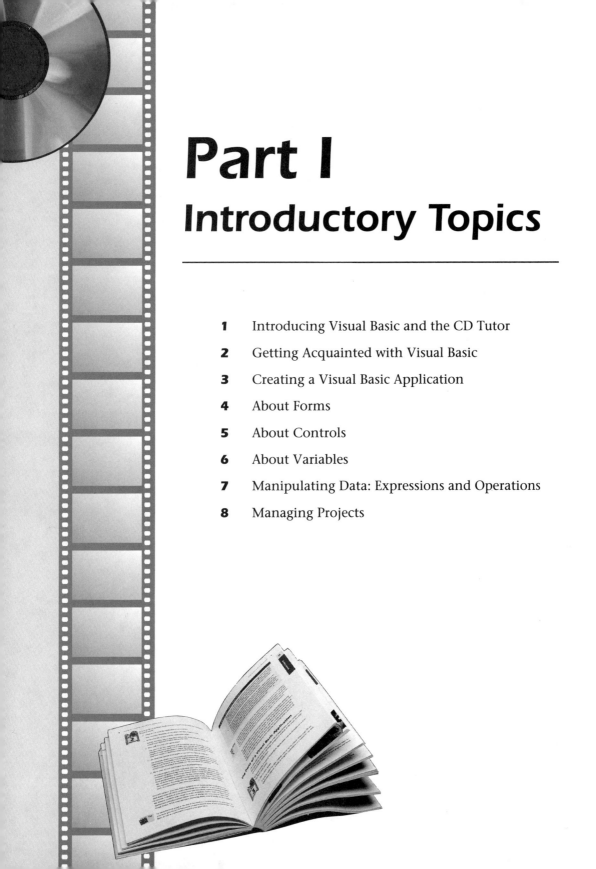

# Part I
## Introductory Topics

## Lesson 1

# Introducing Visual Basic and the CD Tutor

Welcome to Que's *Visual Basic CD Tutor*. This workbook and the accompanying CD offer you a unique, interactive approach to learning Visual Basic, one of the most popular programming products available. Using clear and concise explanations, illustrated examples, and special multimedia demonstrations, Que's *Visual Basic CD Tutor* takes you step-by-step through the process of mastering the fundamentals of Visual Basic. It's like having a complete introductory seminar in a box, but without the high admission price or uncomfortable chairs.

In this introductory lesson, we'll explain a little about Visual Basic, and why it's such an interesting and powerful way to develop programming applications for Microsoft Windows. We'll also show you more about the workbook and the CD Tutor—how to use them, what they contain, and what the various symbols we use signify.

A little bit of familiarity on your part with fundamental programming terms and concepts would be helpful, but is not required. You should know what a programming language is, what constitutes a user interface, and a little bit about programming terms such as variables and procedures. If you're not familiar with these terms, refer to Que's *Computer User's Dictionary*, 5th Edition. More experienced readers may wish to refer to Que's *Computer Programmer's Dictionary* as well.

## About Visual Basic

Microsoft released the first version of Visual Basic in 1991. Intended to offer Windows programmers a powerful but easy-to-use environment for creating programs, Visual Basic combines the simple, straightforward command set of the BASIC programming language with powerful but easily implemented tools for creating Windows-compatible user interfaces. As the foundation for their macros languages, Visual Basic has been integrated into virtually all of Microsoft's own Windows applications, such as Excel and Word for Windows.

 **Note**

What about BASIC itself? The original BASIC (Beginners All-purpose Symbolic Instruction Code) programming language was developed at Dartmouth in the 1960s as an aid for teaching programming. Most other languages in use at the time were cumbersome and even counter-intuitive. What's more, programs had to be translated into instructions the computer could recognize (a process called "compiling") and then had to be submitted to the computer to be run. A mistake in using the programming language—usually called a *syntax error*—didn't become apparent until compilation time. After correcting a little slip, such as a misplaced comma, the poor programming student had to resubmit the entire program.

BASIC, however, was designed to be interactive. This meant that the computer reacted to each new instruction as it was typed. This made it easy to catch syntax errors before a person tried to run a program. It also enabled the programmer to see results almost immediately.

The first version of BASIC was fairly limited in power, but subsequent revisions of the language have extended its scope. Microsoft got started in the 1970s by creating versions of BASIC (among other things) for small computers. The last important small-computer version of BASIC prior to Visual Basic was QBasic, which appeared with DOS 5.0. This version gave BASIC many of the features found in most up-to-date languages, especially advanced structures for making decisions. Visual Basic has expanded this capability even more.

Visual Basic has a couple of important aspects. For one thing, over the last several years you may have heard quite a bit about object-oriented programming (OOP for short)—OOP is definitely a computer industry buzzword. Well, you can think of Visual Basic as an object-oriented form of BASIC, as opposed to procedure-oriented languages such as QBasic.

What's the difference? First, a procedure-based language requires you to write long sequences of programming code to do everything in a program. Not only do you have to write procedures that do all the work, you also must include programming code to draw and enable the parts of the program seen by the user, the *user interface*.

For example, to create a single command button, like the OK button you see on some Windows dialog boxes, you would have to write programming code to draw the button and to determine whether it's been clicked. All this is in addition to the code you must provide to make the button do its work.

In an object-oriented environment such as Visual Basic, on the other hand, you're generally provided a wide range of user interface elements that already have been designed, such as command buttons, scroll bars, and text edit boxes. You don't have to create elements like command buttons from the ground up; you merely have to indicate what should happen to a particular object when, say, a user clicks it. You also have the tools to adjust the appearance of such a button (or any other user interface element), including where it appears on the screen, what color it is, whether it's labeled with a caption, and so on.

By the way, user interface elements such as command buttons and scroll bars are sometimes called *controls*. Together, controls and other items such as windows and dialog boxes are referred to as *objects*—hence the "object" in object-oriented programming. All objects in an OOP environment come with the programming code to draw them and to handle what might happen to them (such as a mouse click) built-in.

This last idea—associating procedures in an object with specific user actions—is the other important point about Visual Basic. In an old style programming language, the program paused at singular points where the user was allowed to do exactly one thing, but Visual Basic, on the other hand, allows for many different procedures to be activated depending on where on the screen a user might click. For example, a user might click any one of several command buttons, might enter text in a text edit book, or could choose a menu command.

A computer language that makes this possible is called an event-driven programming language. Specific user actions, such as pressing a key or clicking the mouse, are referred to as *events*. This event-driven structure is the foundation of Visual Basic, and indeed of Microsoft Windows as a whole.

The really good news is that all the code to handle events at the highest level is built into Visual Basic. When a VB program is running, the system knows when an event has occurred, what kind of event it was, and what object it was associated with. For example, if a user clicks a button, the VB system activates the button and then runs whatever procedure was associated with the mouse click event. The button then performs whatever task it was programmed to do.

The concepts previously described will become increasingly clear as we dive into Visual Basic itself, throughout this workbook and in the multimedia segments of the CD Tutor.

# About the CD Tutor

Perhaps the most important part of this entire package is the Visual Basic tutor contained on the CD-ROM disc accompanying this workbook. Unlike most other book-disc combinations, this workbook is primarily intended to support the CD, not the other way around. Ideally, you should work at your computer with the CD Tutor application running, and with this workbook open.

### Starting the CD Tutor

To run the CD Tutor once it's been installed, locate the Visual Basic CD Tutor group within the Windows Program Manager. Double-click the group icon to open it. Within it you'll see the icon for the Visual Basic CD Tutor application. Double-click this icon to launch the tutor application.

### Installing the CD Tutor

All the files needed to run the CD Tutor application and to display the multimedia segments it contains are stored on the CD that accompanies this workbook. Although most of these files remain on the CD, it's necessary to copy a few of them to your hard disk. The files needed take up about 900K of disk space if you don't have Visual Basic installed on your computer, and about 400K if you do.

 **Note** If you have Visual Basic installed, you can run the CD Tutor application directly from the CD without installing it to your hard drive. This will save about 400K of disk space. Use Program Manager's File, Run command, and enter VBCD3QUE.EXE as the name of the program to run.

If you don't have Visual Basic installed, you'll need to install the CD Tutor application on your hard drive. To make it easy, we've included a setup program on the CD itself. This setup application copies all the files you need to the correct locations on your hard disk, creates a CD Tutor group for the Windows Program Manager, and creates a CD Tutor icon within that group. Figure 1.1 shows what the setup program looks like when it first starts up.

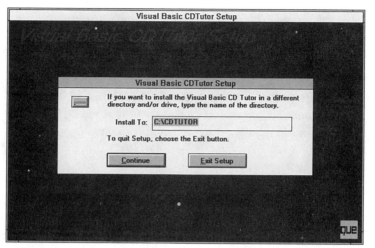

**Figure 1.1**
The CD Tutor Setup application.

Take the following steps to install the Visual Basic CD Tutor Application:

1. Insert the Visual Basic CD Tutor disc into your CD-ROM drive.

2. Choose the Run command from the Windows Program Manager File menu.

3. In the text box under Command Line, type the drive letter for your CD-ROM drive, followed by :\SETUP. Thus, if your CD-ROM drive is D, you'd type:

   **d:\setup**

4. Click the OK button.

5. Follow the on-screen directions in the CD Tutor setup program.

The CD Tutor application makes no assumptions about what drive letter is assigned to your CD-ROM drive, other than that it isn't A or B. (These letters are always reserved for floppy disk drives.) Instead, the Tutor application locates your CD-ROM drive each time it starts up. For this reason, you cannot run the tutorial unless the CD is in place. If you try to run the tutorial without the CD, the Tutor will ask you to insert the CD before you proceed.

Introductory Topics

**Note** The CD Tutor disc must be loaded into your CD-ROM drive before you run the Tutor application for the CD Tutor to function properly. Most of the CD Tutor's information is stored on the disc.

## Using the Components of the CD Tutor

The options available in each part of the tutor are fairly self-explanatory, but are outlined briefly in the following sections.

### Lessons

The tutor contains nineteen *lessons*, each numbered to match a lesson in this workbook. You can view a list of all the lessons by clicking the Lessons button on the main CD Tutor screen. To work with a particular lesson, click the button next to that lesson's name. This will take you to a *lesson screen*.

Within each lesson, there are a number of multimedia *presentations* keyed to specific topics. Each of these presentations is launched from a button on the lesson screen. When you click a presentation's button (only a single-click is required), your computer display shows some part of the Visual Basic interface. You'll see an on-screen demonstration of some aspect of Visual Basic, accompanied by narration played over your computer's speakers.

**Note**     You need a SoundBlaster-compatible sound card to hear the narrated segments.

When you see in the workbook a multimedia icon like the one at the left, that's your cue to click the corresponding icon on the appropriate lesson screen of the CD Tutor. To see how this works, get the CD Tutor up and running on your computer, go to Lesson 1, and click the first multimedia button.

As the segment plays, you'll see a control labeled Lotus ScreenCam in the lower part of your computer screen. Using this control, which works like a VCR's control panel, you can pause, rewind, fast forward, or stop the presentation currently being shown. As soon as a presentation plays to the end, or you stop it, you return to the lesson screen, ready for the next part of that lesson.

**Note** Did you remember to click the button to play multimedia presentation 2 when you saw the icon at the left of the preceding paragraph? (Don't worry—throughout the rest of the workbook, they're usually not this close together...but keep your eyes open, and play the corresponding presentation whenever you encounter an icon.)

### Quizzes

When you've finished a lesson, you can take a quiz to test your mastery of the lesson's subject matter. Each quiz consists of three to five questions. If you click an incorrect answer for any question, you'll be told the correct answer, and given a shot at another variation of the same question. After three incorrect responses, the CD Tutor will suggest that you return to the lesson. Any time your answer is correct, you go on to the next question. When you've answered everything correctly, the Tutor suggests you proceed to the next lesson.

You can exit a quiz at any time by single-clicking the Exit Quiz button at the bottom of the quiz window.

### Interactive Reference

Finally, the Tutor offers an interactive reference to important parts of Visual Basic. When you click the Reference button on the main screen, you'll see a reproduction of the Visual Basic user interface. You can access reference information about any part of the interface, just by clicking it.

Sometimes, there's more than one level of information. For instance, if you click the toolbox, you'll get a general description of what the toolbox is; you also can click a specific tool within the toolbox to access reference information about that tool. Another example of this layering is that if you click a menu name on the menu bar, the full menu drops down, and you then can click any command on that menu to access reference information about the particular command.

After you've read the written description of the item you've clicked, you can click `Play Segment` to launch a multimedia presentation demonstrating how to use that item. Some items don't have multimedia presentations associated with them; in those cases, the `Play Segment` button is dimmed and can't be clicked.

**Caution**   The title bar of the interactive reference window is not part of the interactive reference, and if you click it, you won't get information about Visual Basic's title bar! In fact, because the CD Tutor application uses the interactive reference screen's title bar for its own purposes, you should avoid clicking it while you use the interactive reference. (In case you're wondering, Visual Basic's title bar functions just like any standard Windows title bar, with a control menu at the extreme left, and icons for minimizing and maximizing/restoring at the extreme right.)

### Exiting the CD Tutor

To exit the tutor completely, click the Exit Tutor button at the bottom of the CD Tutor main screen. If you merely wish to exit a particular lesson, you can do so at any time (even before you've viewed all the multimedia segments) by clicking the Return to Lesson List button at the bottom of the lesson screen. You also should do this when you've finished with a lesson and wish to move immediately to the next lesson.

# About the Workbook

This workbook contains nineteen lessons corresponding to the nineteen lessons in the CD Tutor application. Each of the workbook lessons presents an overview of the material contained in the respective lesson, along with definitions, notes, and explanations related to the multimedia segments on the CD-ROM.

As noted earlier, at relevant points within each lesson, you'll find a multimedia icon with a number on it. Whenever you see one, you should click the corresponding button in the CD Tutor to see a multimedia segment tied to that topic.

Some other icons used in the workbook are as follows:

**Note**   This paragraph indicates a note, sort of a sidestep from the regular text. Often, this is some important fact regarding Visual Basic that deserves your focused attention for a moment.

**Tip**   This paragraph clues you in to a nifty—but not totally obvious—fact about Visual Basic, something that will make your programming life easier.

This paragraph identifies a caution regarding some common programming mistake you should avoid, or some preventative action that you need to take.

Key concepts and terms also are summarized at each lesson's end. Each lesson includes ample space for writing notes in the margins, and there are extra pages for making notes at the end of the workbook.

This lesson had three demonstration multimedia presentations. If you haven't viewed any of the presentations yet, please review the instructions in the section "Using the Components of the CD Tutor," earlier in this lesson.

Look at each part of the lesson screen and make sure that you know how the CD Tutor works. When you've done that, you're ready to proceed to the next lesson, where you'll take a closer look at the parts of the Visual Basic development environment.

Now you should be ready for the quiz.

## Lesson 2

# Getting Acquainted with Visual Basic

## Overview

Remember, this workbook is designed to support you as you view presentations in the CD Tutor. To that end, you should have the CD Tutor application up and running on your computer. Whenever you see a multimedia icon such as the one following this paragraph, you should click the appropriately numbered multimedia button for that lesson in the CD Tutor.

In this lesson, we introduce you to Visual Basic itself. By lesson's end we'll have covered the following items:

- ☐ The typical parts of Visual Basic as they appear on your computer after installation

- ☐ How to start Visual Basic

- ☐ What the program looks like once started

- ☐ The different parts of Visual Basic, such as toolboxes and control windows

- ☐ How to get online help, including context-sensitive help, and help for specific topics

**Note** It isn't necessary to have Visual Basic itself running while you're working with this or most of the other lessons in the Visual Basic CD Tutor. The CD Tutor application shows you portions of the Visual Basic environment when necessary.

# The Visual Basic Environment

Now that the preliminaries are over, we can move on to Visual Basic. First, we'll see the parts of a typical Visual Basic installation and how to get the program started.

## Parts of Visual Basic

Visual Basic and its component files and applications appear within the Windows Program Manager in a group named—unless you specified otherwise at installation time—Visual Basic. Figure 2.1 shows what the group generally includes.

**Figure 2.1**
Contents of the Visual Basic group.

*The Visual Basic Group:* A typical Visual Basic installation might include the following:

☐ An icon for Visual Basic

☐ Various files for the online help

☐ A Wizard application to help simplify the creation of an executable application file from an existing project

☐ A Readme file with information that didn't make it into the User Manual before press time

☐ Additional tools, such as Crystal Reports and the Hotspot editor

**Note** You may have noticed that we hedged a good bit when talking about what to expect in the Visual Basic program group. The contents of this group depend on the choices you made when Visual Basic was first installed on your computer.

### Starting Up Visual Basic

In addition to requiring as much as 40 M of hard disk space, Visual Basic needs at least 4 M of RAM to run. (This is true under Windows 3.1; other environments, such as Windows NT, may require more RAM.) If your RAM is limited, it might be a good idea to close any other applications that are running, unless you absolutely need them open, which isn't likely.

To launch Visual Basic, double-click the program's icon within the Visual Basic group.

## The Visual Basic Interface

If you aren't familiar with it, Visual Basic may appear a little daunting at first (see fig. 2.2). There are a lot of things on-screen. However, you'll find these items are logically organized and straightforward to use.

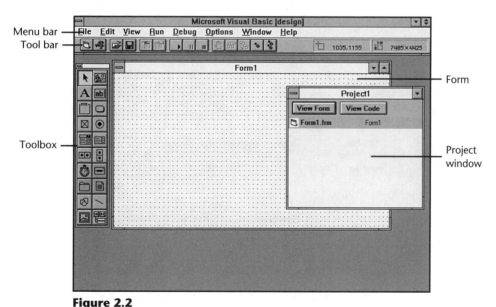

**Figure 2.2**
The basic appearance of the Visual Basic environment.

There are five main parts to the Visual Basic user interface:

☐ The menu bar

☐ The tool bar

☐ The toolbox

☐ The form window

☐ Various other windows, such as the Properties and Project windows

## Menu Bar

As with all Microsoft Windows applications, many (but not all) of Visual Basic's features and functions are contained within the various menus in the menu bar, which appears along the top of the Visual Basic window.

Visual Basic has eight menus of commands, as shown in the following table:

| Menu | Menu Items |
|------|-----------|
| File | General commands for working with Visual Basic projects, including commands to save and print your work |
| Edit | Commands for making changes to a project or to parts thereof |
| View | Commands to control which Visual Basic elements appear on-screen |
| Run | Commands to execute a project |
| Debug | Special options for eliminating Visual Basic errors |
| Options | Options to customize Visual Basic |
| Window | Commands to display or bring to the front certain Visual Basic windows, such as the Project and Properties windows |
| Help | Commands to access online help |

## Tool Bar

The tool bar appears just below the menu bar. You'll find that the buttons along the tool bar correspond to menu commands; the tool bar simply provides a faster and easier way to access the most commonly used commands.

The tool bar includes, from left to right:

| Tool Bar Item | Equivalent Menu Item | Function |
| --- | --- | --- |
| Create new form | New Form in File menu | Add a blank form to the current project |
| Create new module | New Module in File menu | Add an empty code module to the current project |
| Open project | Open Project in File menu | Open an existing Visual Basic project |
| Save current project | Save Project in File menu | Save changes to current project |
| Display Menu Design window | Menu Design in Window menu | Access the Menu Design window to add or edit menu bar for current form |
| Display Properties window | Properties in Window menu | Access the Properties window to change control or form properties |
| Start application | Start in Run menu | Run current project |
| Break application | Break in Run menu | Halt execution of running project, remain in run mode |
| Stop application | End in Run menu | Cease execution of running project, return to design mode |
| Set/Reset breakpoint | Toggle Breakpoint in Debug menu | Set or reset a breakpoint at selected line of code; program stops running when breakpoint encountered |
| Display value of selection | Instant Watch in Debug menu | Show contents of selected expression in Code window |
| Step into program | Single Step in Debug menu | Run program one line at a time; repeat this command for each line to run |
| Step over procedure | Procedure Step in Debug menu | Run program one procedure at a time |

## Toolbox

The toolbox is one of the most important parts of the Visual Basic user interface. In general, controls on the toolbox are used to create and manipulate objects. Recall from the introductory lesson that objects are at the heart of Visual Basic, and include things such as command buttons, text boxes, scroll bars, and so on.

The toolbox should contain the following tools (left to right, top to bottom), as shown in the following table:

| Tool | Purpose |
| --- | --- |
| Pointer | Moves and changes the size of objects |
| Picture box | Creates a frame for a graphic object |
| Label | Creates a frame for a text item; used mainly to label other items, but can function like a command button |
| Text box | Creates a box into which user enters text |
| Frame | Creates a rectangular frame for grouping other controls; controls in a frame are bound to it |
| Command button | Creates a command button that appears to depress when the user clicks it |
| Check box | Creates an option that may be checked or unchecked |
| Option button | Lets the user select one among a number of mutually exclusive choices; usually used in groups |
| Combo box | Creates a control with a text edit box and a list of choices |
| List box | Creates a control with a list of choices only |
| Horizontal scroll bar | Adds a scroll bar for scrolling left and right |
| Vertical scroll bar | Adds a scroll bar for scrolling up and down |
| Timer | Adds a watch for generating events at a specified interval |
| Drive list box | Displays currently available disk drives |
| Directory list box | Displays directories on current drive |
| File list box | Displays files in current directory |
| Shape | Creates a geometric figure |
| Line | Draws lines |

| Tool | Purpose |
|------|---------|
| Image | Creates a frame for a graphics object; functions like a command button |
| Data | Connects to an existing database |

**Note**   Your edition of Visual Basic may support and include additional tools. These appear as icons in the toolbox when they are included in the project file.

## Windows

Next to the toolbox, several windows used in Visual Basic are among its most important features. Visual Basic uses windows to display things such as the properties associated with objects you've created, and the programming code that goes with these objects.

The principle control windows in Visual Basic are shown in the following table:

| Window | Use |
|--------|-----|
| Form | Initially provides the blank canvas onto which objects are placed. (See the following section on the Blank Form.) There is one of these for each form in the project, and each can be shown or hidden as needed. |
| Code | Shows basic programming code associated with various objects and events, or used in stand-alone procedures. There is one of these for each form and also for each module, and each can be shown or hidden as needed. |
| Debug | Tracks execution of current project; used to locate and eliminate errors. The debug window normally is visible when VB is actually executing your program. It can be hidden if need be. |
| Project | Shows all forms and code modules in the current project. Can be used to show a selected form or module. The project window also shows any "add-ins"; these are files such as the Common Dialog control that have the file extension .VBX. The Project window has two command buttons to show form and code windows, or to bring them to the front if hidden or restore them if minimized. |
| Properties | Shows all property settings for the currently selected object; can be used to change them. |

### Blank Form

Finally, there's the "blank canvas" upon which all your Visual Basic work is done. All objects appear on forms; there's at least one form (and up to about 230 forms) per project. The current form appears within a Form Window; you can have more than one form open and visible at once. When more than one form is open, the uppermost is the current form. The current form's title bar is also highlighted. Figure 2.2 showed a blank form.

A form is really just a window; you can add menus and command buttons or other typical window features to it. You'll learn much more about forms in Lesson 4, "About Forms."

So much for the parts of the Visual Basic interface; as mentioned earlier, there's quite a bit to it. Don't worry, though, if you find yourself getting lost. Help is only a keystroke away.

# Getting Help

Visual Basic offers several kinds of online help. In addition to quick help that simply identifies tool icons on-screen, you can immediately access more thorough, context-sensitive help for certain items. In general, you can search through the available help using the help system's table of contents, or you can type in a requested topic to see a list of items matching it.

### Context-Sensitive Help

The easiest way to get help is to press the F1 key with an item selected on-screen. If help exists for that item, Visual Basic displays the help in a window. If no help is available, you'll see an alert box informing you of that fact. Figure 2.3 shows context-sensitive help for the toolbox.

### Getting Help by Topic

To view the table of contents of the help system, choose the Contents command from the Visual Basic Help menu. You'll see a screen similar to Figure 2.4.

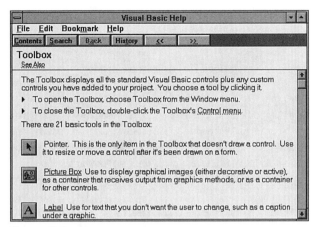

**Figure 2.3**

Context-sensitive help.

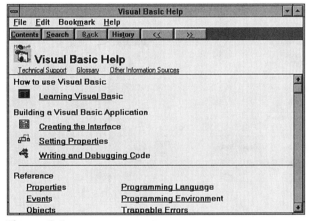

**Figure 2.4**

The help system's topics screen.

The mouse pointer changes to a hand when you move it over topics for which help is available. To access help, follow these steps:

1. Choose Contents from the Help menu.

2. Move the mouse pointer over the topic for which you want help.

3. Click the topic.

   A list of subtopics appears in a separate window.

4.  Find the specific topic for which you want help.

5.  Click the subtopic's name.

Specific help appears in another window.

**Note**    Within the help for a topic, certain words or phrases appear with either a dotted or a solid underline. You can find help immediately for one of these items by clicking it. Single-click a dotted underline to show a definition of the underlined term in a popup window. Clicking a solid underlined term takes you to the help for that topic.

## Searching for Help Subjects

If you know what you're looking for, there's a faster way to search for help than relying on the table of contents. You can type a specific subject name and have Visual Basic search for topics that match. Figure 2.5 shows the Search window.

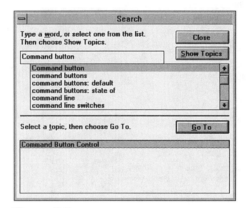

**Figure 2.5**
Searching for help by specified topic.

To find help on a specific subject, follow these steps:

1.  Choose Search for Help on... from the Help menu.

The Search window appears.

2.  Type in the text box the topic for which you want help.

3.  Click Show Topics.

A list of available topics appears in the box at the bottom of the window.

4. Click a topic to select it.

5. Click the GoTo button. Help for the topic appears in a separate window.

### Navigating within the Help System

In addition to seeing cross-referenced help on other topics (by clicking words or phrases that have a dotted underline), you also can move around the help system with other controls (see fig. 2.6).

**Figure 2.6**
Help Window controls to move around within the help system.

Help controls and their functions are shown in the following table:

| Control | Function |
| --- | --- |
| Contents | Return to Help Table of Contents screen |
| Search | Return to Help Search screen |
| Back | Go back to last topic viewed, if any |
| History | Select from among all topics viewed this session |
| << | Go back one topic or page in alphabetical listing |
| >> | Go forward one topic or page in alphabetical listing |

# Review

In this lesson we introduced Visual Basic, looked at its user interface, and saw how to get online help. Points covered included:

☐ Visual Basic contains several components, generally to be found in the Visual Basic group.

☐ You start Visual Basic by double-clicking its icon, as you would any Windows application.

☐ Important parts of the Visual Basic interface include the menu bar, the tool bar, the toolbox, and various control windows.

☐ It's easy to get online help, including context-sensitive help, and help for specific topics. Context-sensitive help is available by pressing the F1 key. The Help menu contains commands for accessing help through the table of contents, or by specifying a topic.

**Quiz**

Now you should be ready for the quiz.

# Creating a Visual Basic Application

## Overview

In this lesson we'll take you step by step through the process of creating a very simple Visual Basic application. Even if your programming experience is limited, you'll be surprised by how easy it is to get something up and running in Visual Basic. Granted, we won't be showing you anything very grand, but even this limited exercise should give you an appreciation of the relatively simple and straightforward way in which you design applications in Visual Basic.

In this lesson, we'll look at the following:

☐ What you should do before you start

☐ The parts of a Visual Basic application, including forms, controls, and their associated procedures

☐ How to create a Visual Basic application in three broad steps: designing the interface, defining properties and procedures, and preparing an executable file

## Before You Start: Application Planning

There's an old saying: "Well-begun is half done." Nowhere is this more true than in programming. While you can go pretty far programming by the seat of your pants—especially in a highly supportive environment like Visual Basic—you'll get much more done in much less time if you start out in your friendly neighborhood word processor, or even with pencil and paper.

As you sit down to begin work on a new application, keep the following things in mind:

☐ *What do you want the application to accomplish?*

This includes thinking about what you *don't* want it to do.

☐ *With what sort of data will the application work?*

Strictly numeric data is handled differently than character data, and mixed-type data is handled differently still.

☐ *Who will be using your application?*

The answer to this question will determine much about the sort of user interface you need. Obviously, you can get away with something simpler if your application is solely for private use, whereas an application you mean to distribute will need to look and act nicer.

☐ *Are there any actions that might be repeated in different contexts?*

An example might be a financial calculation that's performed in two or more places. Especially if these repeat actions are central to your application, you'll want to design it in a way that lets you program any such action once, making it available for use anywhere it's needed.

☐ *Have parts of your application been developed before?*

As you progress, you may find that you can "borrow" pieces from previous programming work. Even if you're a novice, though, you can borrow capability, both from Visual Basic's built-in functions and from programming examples, in the online help. (We'll have more to say on both these subjects toward the end of the Tutor.) You might also consider checking out the appropriate forums in online services such as CompuServe and America Online.

For each project, you may find it helpful to sit down at the word processor and make yourself some notes regarding these subjects. It also can be helpful to prepare a sketch of your proposed user interface, concentrating mainly on the kind of controls you mean to make available, rather than on their exact appearance and placement—these sorts of things are very easy to adjust in Visual Basic. With your advance planning done, you're ready to dive right in.

**Tip** Try using the blank pages at the end of this book as a central location for your notes. As your work goes on, you'll find you've created a kind of diary of your progress with Visual Basic, as well as a permanent record of your good ideas.

Introductory Topics

## In Days of Yore... About Flow Charts

There was a time when a serious student of computer programming would never think of starting work on a new application without first preparing a flow chart. Your humble author had drilled into him as a college undergraduate the necessity of preparing such a document, in programming classes where no credit was granted unless an acceptably formatted flow chart was submitted prior to programming.

The younger and the less experienced among you may be asking: What's a flow chart, and why was it so important? In brief, a flow chart is a graphical representation of a computer program's execution. Boxes and other symbols represented important stages in the program's progress (or flow—hence the name). Lines connected stages that followed each other. In effect, a flow chart was another way of expressing a program's *algorithm*, which is a fancy word for a step-by-step procedure. A properly executed flow chart was thought to make it easy to evaluate the potential success of a given algorithm, and to make it easier to translate that algorithm into programming code.

So why was such a useful tool omitted from the pre-application planning suggestions previously given? It's simple: they're no longer that useful. Flow charts were more suited to the old style of interrupt-driven programming, where a program performed a few steps and then paused, waiting for the user to do something, or, more often than not, simply performed a set of actions on a large collection of data without interacting with a user at all.

In an event-driven programming system such as Visual Basic, it really isn't possible to specify the overall flow of an application program, although it might be possible to prepare such diagrams for the application's constituent parts. With the kinds of programming and testing tools available in Visual Basic, however, even such limited flow charts are of questionable utility. The bottom line: You've got better (and more productive) things to do with your programming time than preparing flow charts. Would that it always had been so!

# The Parts of a Visual Basic Application

The first part of a recipe is generally a list of ingredients. In like manner, the first part of our plan for creating a program is to look at the parts of a typical Visual Basic application.

In broad terms, a typical Visual Basic application can be thought of as having three main parts:

☐ One or more **forms**

A form is, as we've said, a blank canvas upon which other parts of an application appear. A form is roughly equivalent to a window—in fact, it can be made to be exactly equivalent to a window.

☐ One or more **controls**

A control is something with which the user interacts, such as a command button or a scroll bar.

☐ One or more **procedures**

A procedure is a sequence of program steps that accomplishes a specific task. There may be procedures associated with each object (form or control) in the application.

## Forms

Any Visual Basic application has at least one form, although it may have several (as many as 230, although, practically speaking, the limit is closer to 35). Figure 3.1 shows a blank form.

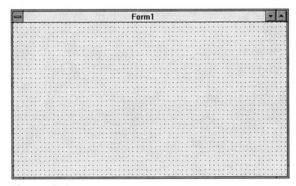

**Figure 3.1**
A blank form.

You have a good bit of flexibility available to you when it comes to specifying how a form should look. Among the items you can change are:

☐ The form's overall size

☐ Whether it can be shrunk to an icon (*minimized*) and expanded to the full size of the screen (*maximized*)

☐ Whether it has a border, and of what type

☐ The form's background color, if any

☐ Where it appears on-screen when activated

You'll learn more about the particulars of these options in Lesson 4, "About Forms."

## Controls

A Visual Basic application consisting of a blank form is of no particular use, even if it happens to contain a lot of programming code. You must give the user some way to interact with the application's innards, and to specify what to do. You accomplish this by using controls. Figure 3.2 shows four controls on a Visual Basic form.

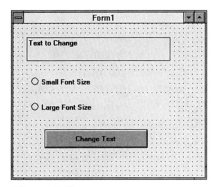

**Figure 3.2**
Four controls: a command button, two option buttons, and a text box.

In addition to choosing what sorts of controls to use, you also can specify a number of different things about the individual controls themselves, as you can with forms. These include (but by no means are limited to) the following items:

☐ Where a control appears on a form

☐ Whether the control has a *caption*; in other words, a word or phrase identifying it to the user

☐ The control's size

☐ Its background color, if any

In addition, there are qualities specific to individual control types. We'll talk about all these things in Lesson 5, "About Controls."

**Note** An important thing to keep in mind is the relationship of controls to forms in Visual Basic. A control always belongs to the form on which it appears. In technical jargon, we say that the control is the child of the form, and that the form is the control's parent. This doesn't mean you can't move a control from one form to another, but it does affect how you refer to a particular control—generally, a control's parent form is part of its overall name.

## Procedures

A Visual Basic application with well-designed forms containing lots of controls might look nice, but without programming code it won't do much. This code resides in procedures, which are usually associated with individual objects (forms or controls) and with different things (events) that might happen to them. Figure 3.3 shows the Visual Basic Code Window with a small procedure written in it.

Here are a few things to keep in mind about procedures:

☐ Procedures are where the application's work gets done

☐ Any procedure defined for a particular object (a given form or command button, for example) belongs to that object alone

☐ Procedures consist of statements written in Visual Basic's specific flavor of the BASIC programming language

You'll learn about the various Visual Basic statements in Lesson 7, "Manipulating Data: Expressions and Operations."

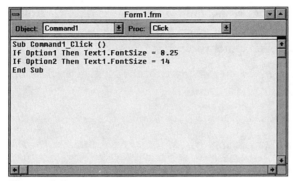

**Figure 3.3**
A procedure associated with a command button.

# A Visual Basic Application in Three Steps

Having seen the various parts that go into a typical Visual Basic application, you're now ready to look at how to create such an application. We'll do so through the medium of a very simple program—one that does no more than print a message when you click one button, and quit when you click the other.

To create this application, we follow three basic steps:

1. We design the user interface. This includes determining the size of the application's form, and the number, nature, size, and placement of its controls.

2. We "fill in" the application's objects. To do so, we specify certain qualities possessed by these objects. We call these qualities *properties*. We also specify procedures for some of the objects.

3. We create an executable application. After testing to make sure it works as we want, we make an EXE file that can be run from the Microsoft Windows Program Manager.

## Designing the Interface

We start out with the following specification, obtained from our pre-application planning. We want an application with two buttons. If the user clicks the first, the program displays a message. If the user clicks the other, the program quits. That's all.

From the above, we determine that we need three controls: two command buttons, and a place in which to display a message. All of these controls occupy a single, appropriately sized form.

To implement the user interface for the Message application, follow these steps:

1. Start Visual Basic.

   A blank form appears.

2. Click the command button tool on the toolbox.

3. Position the mouse pointer over the blank form in roughly the place the button should be. Click and drag out the button, making it about an inch wide and a third that tall. Release the mouse button.

4. Repeat Steps 2 and 3 to draw a second command button below the first.

5. Click the Label tool in the toolbox.

6. Position the mouse pointer over the form, above the two buttons. Click and drag out a label about three inches long and half an inch high. Release the mouse button.

7. Adjust the position of the three controls. Click a control to select it, then click and drag it to a new position, if needed.

8. Click and drag the lower-right corner of the form to make it smaller.

That's all there is to it! Figure 3.4 shows the proposed interface for the Message application.

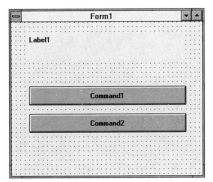

**Figure 3.4**
The user interface for the Message application, in progress.

## Defining Object Properties and Procedures

As they are now, the two buttons and the label on this application are inadequate. For one thing, they have boring names (Command1, Command2, and Label1). Secondly, they don't know yet how to do what we want them to do.

### Properties

First, let's do something about those names. The label should be blank, for now, while the two buttons have names describing their functions. An object's name is one of many properties it has, and you can adjust these properties in the Properties window (see fig. 3.5).

**Figure 3.5**
The Properties window, showing properties for the button Command1.

The following steps show what's involved in changing the names of the three control objects on the Message application:

1. We click the label to select it. Then, we choose Properties from the Visual Basic Window menu.

   The Properties window appears.

2. We locate the Caption property, which determines how an object is labeled. We select the text and press the Backspace key, erasing it. The text disappears on the label object as well. To save this change, we click the checkmark icon at the top of the Properties window.

3. We click to select the first command button, then access the Properties window again (Shortcut: Press the F4 key). We change the caption to Message by selecting the Caption property, then typing **Message** in the edit box at the top of the properties window. We click the checkmark icon to save the change.

4. We click to select the second command button. Accessing the Properties window, we change the button's caption to Quit.

5. We double-click the Properties window's Control menu icon to close it for now.

Figure 3.6 shows what the Message application looks like after these changes have been made.

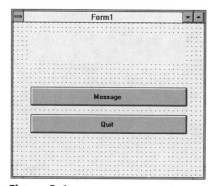

**Figure 3.6**
Message application objects with the appropriate captions.

**Procedures**

Believe it or not, all that remains to do is tell the two command buttons what to do when the user clicks either of them. The appropriate procedures are defined in the Code window for each object. You access the Code window for an object by double-clicking the object. Figure 3.7 shows the Code window for the button that is labeled Message.

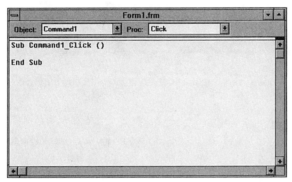

**Figure 3.7**
The Code window, ready to program the Message button.

The following list outlines how to enable the two command buttons:

1.  Start with the easiest. Double-click the button now labeled Quit. The Code window appears.

2.  Type **End** at the present cursor location. Double-click the Code window's control menu icon.

    This completes the programming for the Quit button.

3.  Double-click the button labeled Message. Enter this line:

    ```
    Label1.Caption = "This is what I really call a message!"
    ```

    This line of code resets the label control's Caption property. Resetting properties within code is at the heart of Visual Basic programming.

4.  Double-click the Code window's control menu icon again to close it.

Figure 3.8 shows what the Code window looks like after these two lines have been entered.

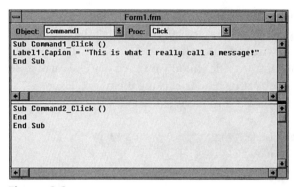

**Figure 3.8**
The Code window, showing the code for both command buttons.

### Debugging

That's all there is to it! But how do we know it works? The fact is, we *don't* know that it works; at least, not yet. This isn't hard to verify, however, and if it didn't work for some reason, it wouldn't be hard to fix.

**Running a Program** It's the simplest thing in the world to run a Visual Basic application at any point during the design process. All you have to do is select the Start command from the Visual Basic Run menu. (Alternatively, you can press F5 on your keyboard, or click the Start button on the tool bar.) Figure 3.9 shows what happens when you do this within the developing Message application.

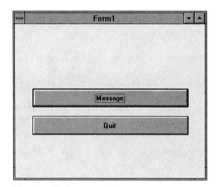

**Figure 3.9**
Running the message application within Visual Basic.

Following are some things to have in mind when running a work in progress:

☐ Visual Basic remains visible, but isn't fully active unless something— such as an error—causes the program to stop.

☐ You can drag the application's form around on the screen. You also can minimize the default kind of form down to an icon. (More about this in Lesson 4, "About Forms.")

☐ You don't have to rely on your application to quit. (It is, however, considered bad form not to include some way to quit within your application.) To stop it for good, choose End from the Visual Basic Run menu. You also can double-click the Control menu icon on the application's form.

**Fixing Problems** Things go wrong. There's no problem with the Message application; however, if an error were encountered during program execution, Visual Basic would inform us of the problem via a dialog box, as shown in Figure 3.10.

**Figure 3.10**
A dialog box saying that there's a problem.

What do we do then? The only thing to do, really, is to click the OK button on the dialog box. Doing so brings up the Code window for the procedure where the problem occurred (see fig. 3.11).

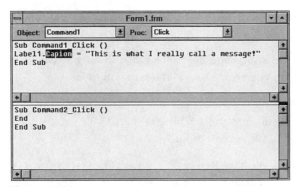

**Figure 3.11**
The Code window, identifying the problem with the Message program.

Aha! A typographical error. Visual Basic doesn't like it when you leave letters out of properties' names. We add the missing "t" directly in the Code window, and then choose Continue from the Visual Basic Run menu (or press F5). Figure 3.12 shows the results after the Message button has been clicked.

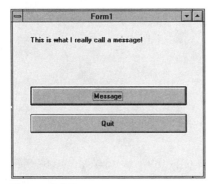

**Figure 3.12**
The Message program now works.

## Preparing and Running an Executable File

Having confirmed that the Message program works, all that remains is to put it into a form that can be used without running Visual Basic itself. To do that, you must create an executable file—one with the extension EXE. Visual Basic has a command to do this.

The command to create an executable file is the Make EXE File command in the Visual Basic File menu. Some things you should know are:

☐ You can run your new application outside Visual Basic, using the Windows Program Manager's Run command (File Menu).

☐ You may create an icon for the new application, and add it to any group you like. Use the Program Manager's New command in its File menu.

☐ Your application will require a special additional file (VBRUN300.DLL) to run on a computer that doesn't have Visual Basic installed. The Setup Wizard, described in Lesson 19, "Simplifying Application Creation," handles this sort of thing for you.

# Review

It isn't, perhaps, as easy as 1-2-3, but this lesson has shown how little work it can take to design and implement a simple Visual Basic program. Along the way, you learned:

☐ The best way to start is by planning an application ahead of time, including how it should look and what it should do.

☐ A Visual Basic application has three main parts: forms, upon which everything else appears; controls, through which the user interacts with the program; and associated procedures, which define (in BASIC) how to do the work.

☐ There are three steps to creating a Visual Basic application: designing the interface, defining properties and procedures for the interface objects, and preparing an executable file.

Now you should be ready for the quiz.

# About Forms

## Overview

In Visual Basic, everything starts with forms. Forms provide the foundation upon which you build your Visual Basic applications. They're the stuff from which windows are made, for one thing. They also can be used to create dialog boxes. This lesson shows you what forms are about, and how to work with them in the Visual Basic context.

This lesson covers the following topics relating to forms:

- ☐ Adding forms to an application

- ☐ Managing forms within an application

- ☐ Using forms from other projects

- ☐ Removing forms from the current project

- ☐ Form properties

- ☐ Form procedures

## Creating and Manipulating Forms

You don't have to add the first form to a new application; Visual Basic starts with an empty form named Form1 in place. At times, though, you'll find it necessary to add one or more extra forms so that your application can present different groups of options to the user. For example, you might have an application with one form that presents a main menu of choices, and additional forms that correspond to each of the choices the user might make (such as viewing a lesson, taking a quiz, looking up reference material—sound familiar?).

Once you have two or more forms in place within an application, you need some way to manage them. If a particular form isn't open, then you need to be able to call it up somehow to work on it. Visual Basic makes it easy to add and keep track of forms within a developing application.

**Note**    Visual Basic calls the set of files that make up an application a *project*; we'll also call it that.

## New Forms

Adding a new form to a project requires this simple set of steps:

1. Make sure you're in Visual Basic; have open the project to which you want to add a form. (Use the Open Project command in the Visual Basic File menu if necessary.)

2. Choose New Form from the File menu, or click the Form icon on the tool bar. Results of doing so are shown in Figure 4.1.

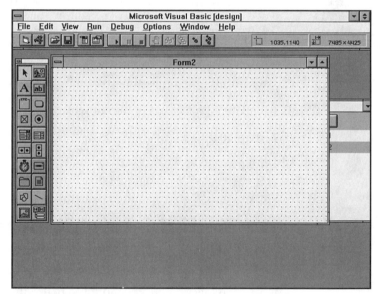

**Figure 4.1**
A new project with a second form added.

3. The new form may completely cover the old one, but you can drag the new one aside to make both visible.

**Note**   Only one form is *active*—that is, capable of being modified—at a time. The active form's title bar appears in inverse video. In Figure 4.1, Form2 is the active form. Click anywhere in a form to make it active if it isn't already.

A new form appears in a separate window. If at any time you want to close a form (without deleting it, of course), just double-click the Control menu icon on its window.

## The Project Window

Whenever you add a new form to a project, it immediately appears in the Project window. The Project window usually is open by default; that is, it's open unless you tell Visual Basic to close it. Figure 4.2 shows the Project window as it appears after the addition of a single new form to a new project.

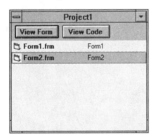

**Figure 4.2**
The Project window, showing two forms in this project.

   To display the Project window, perform the following steps:

1. Have the appropriate project open.

2. Choose Project from the Window menu.

3. The Project window appears, listing all the files contained in the current project.

**Note** If the Project window has been opened, but isn't at the front, click anywhere inside it to make it active and bring it fully forward. This applies to any window within the Microsoft Windows environment. The safest place to click a window is on its title bar or border because nothing changes within the selected window.

By the way, the active window is said to have the *focus*. Any item possessing the focus will be the recipient of any keystrokes the user enters. Focus is an important concept, both in Microsoft Windows and Visual Basic.

### Opening a Form for Editing

You use the Project window to open forms that are closed.

To open a closed form, follow these steps:

1. Display the Project window.

2. Click to select the name of the form you want to open.

3. Click the View Form button on the Project window. The form opens out in a form window as before.

**Tip** You can open a closed form just by double-clicking its name in the Project window.

### Removing a Form from a Project

If you accidentally add a form that you don't need, or if you find that a form you added previously doesn't suit your purposes any longer, you easily can delete it from the current project.

To remove a form from a project, perform the following steps:

1. Display the Project window.

2. Click to select the name of the form you want to remove.

3. Choose the Remove File command from the Visual Basic File menu. If you have made any changes to the form that haven't been saved (using either the Save File or Save Project command in the File menu), then a dialog box appears asking whether you want to save changes (see fig. 4.3). Click the appropriate choice.

**Figure 4.3**
The dialog box that asks if you want to save changes to a form prior to removing it from a project.

4. The form is removed from the project. Its window (if open) closes and its name disappears from the Project window.

**Note** A form removed this way is merely eliminated from the current project; if it was previously saved to your hard disk, it's still there. If you want to permanently remove it from the hard disk, you need to use Windows File Manager's Delete command. If you use Visual Basic's Remove File command on a new form that you've neither saved nor edited, however, that form disappears immediately from the current project *and* from your computer.

### Adding an Existing Form

If a saved form isn't deleted from your computer when you remove it from a project, that implies that the form remains available for later use. In fact, you can add a formerly used form, or a form currently used in another project, if you want. This is one way to save yourself a lot of work.

**Note** Even the most generic of forms might cause problems when added to a new project in the way just described. Of particular concern are relationships the newly added form may have had with other items in the original project. It's important to keep track of everything needed by the form, and to supply it to the new project. Lesson 19, "Simplifying Application Creation," shows ways to do this.

To add a previously created form to the current project, do the following:

1. Choose Add File from the Visual Basic File menu. The Add File dialog box appears (see fig. 4.4).

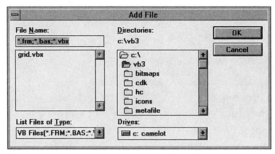

**Figure 4.4**
The Add File dialog box, which enables you to import previously saved items
from other projects.

2. Navigate in the drive, directory, and file lists until you locate the name of the form you want to add.

3. Click to select the form's name.

4. Click OK. The form is added to the current project and is listed in the Project window.

**Caution.** Any modifications you make to a form "borrowed" from another project will affect that project as well! This might "break" the other project. To avoid this, save a copy of the newly added form under a different name. Open the form and make it active, then choose the Save File As command from the Visual Basic file menu. The new copy entirely replaces the old one in the current project.

# Adjusting Forms

Once you've added a form, there are a number of things you can do to bend it to your will. You can change many of its properties, including its size, its position, and even the kind of window it presents when your program is run.

## Resizing a Form

The simplest thing to do to a form is to change its size because a Visual Basic form has sizing handles just like any window does. Figure 4.5 shows a form resizing operation in progress.

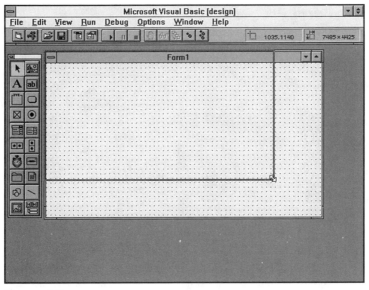

**Figure 4.5**
Changing the size of a form is a simple click-and-drag operation.

To change the size of a form, follow these steps:

1. Use the Project window to display the appropriate form, if it isn't already open and active.

2. Move the mouse pointer over the form's lower-right corner. It turns into a diagonal, double-headed arrow like that shown in Figure 4.5.

3. Click and drag the corner in the appropriate direction: up and left to make the form smaller, down and right to make it larger.

4. Release the mouse button when you've dragged the form to the desired size.

 **Tip**   To change a form's vertical or horizontal size only, move the mouse pointer over the form's bottom edge, then click and drag to make the form taller or shorter. Move the pointer over the form's right edge, then click and drag to make it wider or narrower.

## Form Properties

Size is not the only quality possessed by a form, to be sure. In fact, there's an entire range of properties that belong to any given form. You can view— and possibly change—these properties using the Properties window (see fig. 4.6).

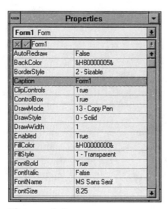

**Figure 4.6**
The Properties window, showing the current properties of Form1.

To view the properties for a given form, follow these steps:

1. Display the form whose properties you want to examine.

2. Choose the Properties command from the Visual Basic Window menu, or press F4 on your keyboard.

3. The Properties window appears, displaying the form's current property settings.

You can drag out the Properties window's sizing handle to view more properties at a time, and see each more fully. You still may need to scroll to view all the form's properties. Double-click the Control menu icon to close the Properties window.

### Form Properties in General

There are a lot of form properties, but don't worry. You might never have occasion to use some of them, and those you will need to use are straight-forward to set.

**Note**  Although it's appropriate to reset certain form properties using the Properties window—such as a form's style and color—other items really should be changed dynamically within the execution of your Visual Basic program. Much, if not all, of a Visual Basic program's work is done in just this way. You'll learn more about this process in Lesson 7, "Manipulating Data: Expressions and Operations."

Some of the more important form properties are shown in the following table:

| Property | Function |
| --- | --- |
| BackColor | Sets the form's background color |
| BorderStyle | Controls the overall type of form shown (see the later section, "Form Types: The BorderStyle Property") |
| Caption | Sets the text to use on the form's title bar |
| Control Box | Sets whether a control box appears on the form |
| Font | Sets the font name, style, and size to use in the form's caption |
| ForeColor | Sets the form's foreground color, using the color palette |
| MaxButton | Sets whether to display a Maximize button on the form's window during program execution |
| MinButton | Sets whether to display a Minimize button on the form's window during program execution |
| MousePointer | Selects one of several available mouse pointers to use when the pointer is over the form |
| Name | Sets the form's name |
| Picture | Loads a graphic into the form; depending on its size, the graphic may fill all or part of the form, with controls drawn on the form appearing in front of the graphic |
| Visible | Sets whether a form can be seen and worked with during program execution |

**Tip**  The best way to see what these various options do is to experiment with them in Visual Basic. Try changing property settings to see the effect each has; you needn't save your work.

In terms of how you set them, form properties fall into two broad classes: those for which you enter a text item, and those from which you choose from an option list or dialog box. You can tell which type of property you're dealing with by looking at the top of the Properties window. In a text property, the drop-down arrow next to the property setting is dimmed. For an option list property, the drop-down arrow is active. For a property set by way of a dialog box, the drop-down arrow becomes an ellipsis.

To change a text item property, do the following:

1. Select the appropriate form and display the Properties window.

2. Click to select the name of the property you want to change.

3. Type the new value for the property in the edit box at the top of the Properties window.

4. Click the checkmark icon to the left of the edit box to save the change you made.

5. Double-click the Properties window's Control menu icon to close it, if desired.

Rather than entering text, some form properties require you to make a choice from among available options. These options may be presented by way of an option list that drops down when you click a pointer icon in the Properties window. Certain properties, such as the Picture property, require you to specify a file's location using a dialog box. These properties are labeled with an ellipsis. Figures 4.7 and 4.8 show both such alternatives.

| Properties | |
|---|---|
| Form1  Form | |
| X ✓ 2 - Sizable | |
| AutoR | 0 - None |
| BackC | 1 - Fixed Single |
| Borde | 2 - Sizable |
| | 3 - Fixed Double |
| Caption | Form1 |
| ClipControls | True |
| ControlBox | True |
| DrawMode | 13 - Copy Pen |
| DrawStyle | 0 - Solid |
| DrawWidth | 1 |
| Enabled | True |
| FillColor | &H00000000& |
| FillStyle | 1 - Transparent |
| FontBold | True |
| FontItalic | False |
| FontName | MS Sans Serif |
| FontSize | 8.25 |

**Figure 4.7**
Choosing a setting for the BorderStyle property from an option list.

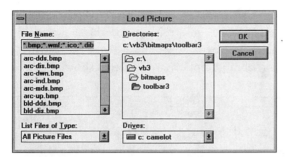

**Figure 4.8**
Choosing a setting for the Picture property with a dialog box.

To change a property for which there is a choice, follow these steps:

1. Select the appropriate form and display the Properties window.

2. Click to select the name of the property you want to change.

3. Click the drop-down list icon to the right of the property's setting in the edit box at the top of the Properties window.

4. The list drops down to display available choices, or opens to display a dialog box.

5. In an option list, click the name of the choice you want. In a dialog box, use the drive, directory, and file lists to navigate to where the file you want to use (for example, a bitmap or icon file) is located, click to select its name, then click OK.

6. Click the checkmark icon to the left of the edit box to save changes.

7. Double-click the Properties window's Control menu icon to close it, if desired.

 **Note** For a property set with the Open File dialog box: If you set the property at design time, as previously described, a copy of the item is taken into your program; you don't need the original. If, on the other hand, your program sets the property at run time, the original item is not taken into your Visual Basic project; it remains in its previous location on your hard disk. If the original item is changed outside of your project, you'll see the change in your project the next time you open it. If you move the item, however, Visual Basic won't be able to find it, and will tell you so, in an error message, when your program runs.

### Form Types: The BorderStyle Property

The BorderStyle property may seem innocuous, but actually its job is crucial: it determines the exact sort of form that appears when you run your program. There are four options available, as shown in Figure 4.9.

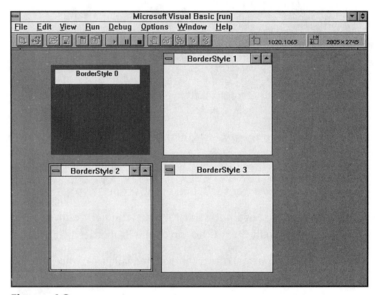

**Figure 4.9**
The four available form types; each has a different BorderStyle property setting. BorderStyle 0 has an invisible title bar and border.

The four form types available are shown in the following table:

| Border Style | Attributes |
| --- | --- |
| 0—None | This form's title and border are invisible; the form cannot be moved or resized |
| 1—Fixed Single | This form can be moved, maximized, and minimized, but cannot be resized; the border is a single line |
| 2—Sizable | This form can be moved, maximized, minimized, and resized. This is the default style, which every form has when first created; the border is a double line |
| 3—Fixed Double | This form can be moved, but cannot be maximized, minimized, or resized; the border is double when the form has the focus |

# Form Procedures

Forms have more than just properties governing their appearance. A form
also may have procedures associated with it, although this is not necessary.
A form's procedures define, in the Visual Basic language, what to do when
various events happen to the form.

## A Few Words about Events

Recall that an event is generated when the program user performs some
action, such as clicking the mouse or pressing a key. (An event also can be
generated by the program itself, but that isn't important now.) It's possible
to associate a procedure—a list of Visual Basic program steps to perform—
for every event associated with a form.

A summary of some of the more important events associated with forms is
shown in the following table:

| Event | Action |
| --- | --- |
| Activate | Form becomes the active form |
| Click | User clicks the form |
| DblClick | User double-clicks the form |
| KeyPress | User presses a key on the keyboard with the form active |
| Load | Form is first placed into memory |
| Unload | Form receives command to remove itself from memory |

You'll learn more about events and event procedures as the book progresses.
Think back to the Message application example from Lesson 3, "Creating a
Visual Basic Application"—the two command buttons each had one procedure associated with their Click event, and the form had no procedures
associated with it.

## Defining Procedures for a Form

You define event procedures for a form using the Visual Basic Code window.
Figure 4.10 shows the Code window for the current form. Note in particular
the Proc drop-down list for events; this is how you create a particular event
procedure, by choosing the event you want to define from this list.

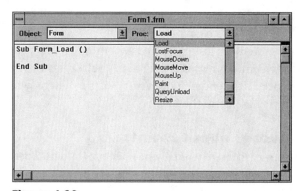

**Figure 4.10**
The Code window for Form1, opened, with the Proc list dropped down.

**Note** Of particular importance is the way Visual Basic refers to defined event procedures. A procedure always has a name. For an event procedure, this name includes the object type it belongs to, with the event the procedure is defined for as a suffix.

To define a form procedure for a specific event, complete the following steps:

1. Display the Project window. Select the appropriate form and then click the View Code button.
   The Code window appears.

2. Choose the appropriate event from the Proc drop-down list. Opening and closing statements for the procedure appear in the Code window, with the text insertion point appearing on a blank line between them.

3. Type the necessary Visual Basic program code to define the procedure.

4. Double-click the Code window's Control menu icon to close the window.

**Tip** Save your work often! Use the Save Project command in the Visual Basic File menu to save changes to all parts of the current project; choose Save File in the same menu to save changes only to the active file.

# Review

In this lesson, you learned the following:

- ☐ You add new forms to an application by using the New Form command in the File menu, or by clicking the Form icon on the Visual Basic tool bar.

- ☐ You manage existing forms using the Project window, which you access using the Project command in the Visual Basic Window menu.

- ☐ You can add an existing form from another project to the current project. You do so using the Add File command in the File menu.

- ☐ You remove a form from a project using the Remove File command in the File menu. This does not erase the form from the hard disk if it previously was saved there.

- ☐ Forms have a number of properties associated with them, which determine how they look and behave. You can change form properties using the Properties window, which you access using the Properties command on the Visual Basic Window menu, or by pressing F4. Form properties may be set within any procedure as part of program execution.

- ☐ One important form property is the BorderStyle property. The four available settings for this property determine the form window's appearance during program execution.

- ☐ A form may have Visual Basic programming language procedures associated with certain events that happen to it. Event procedures are defined using the Code window, which can be accessed with a button on the Project window, by choosing Code from the View menu, by double-clicking the object for which you want to define a procedure, or by pressing F7.

**Quiz**    Now you should be ready for the quiz.

## Lesson 5

# About Controls

## Overview

If forms are the foundation upon which you build a Visual Basic application, then controls provide the framework. Presuming you've worked at all with Microsoft Windows and applications it supports, then you've worked with controls. Command buttons, menus, scroll bars—all of these are controls. They provide the essential components of an application's user interface, dictating how the user interacts with a program and makes it do what he or she wants it to.

This lesson covers the following points regarding controls:

☐ How to add new controls to an application, and how to move, resize, and group them once they're there

☐ What the various control properties are, and how to change them

☐ How to define control procedures

## Creating and Manipulating Controls

You'll find that creating new controls and manipulating existing ones doesn't differ fundamentally from working with forms. One difference to keep in mind is that controls are drawn on forms and *always* belong to the form on which they're drawn. We defined this fact in Lesson 3, "Creating a Visual Basic Application," as a parent-child relationship. A new control is always added to the active form and becomes a child of that form.

## Adding New Controls

When you want to add a new control to a project, you go to the toolbox. Normally, the toolbox is visible. If it isn't, choose Toolbox from the Visual Basic Window menu to make it so. Figure 5.1 shows the toolbox in action.

 ── Command button

**Figure 5.1**
The toolbox, with the Command button control selected.

 Adding a new control to a project follows this simple set of steps:

1. Make sure you're in Visual Basic; have open the project to which you want to add a control. (Use the Open Project command in the Visual Basic File menu, if necessary.)

2. Click the toolbox to select the icon for the tool you want to add.

3. Click anywhere on the form to which you want to add the tool, and drag out the tool. Release the mouse button. The tool appears.

 **Note**    Only one control is *active*—capable of being modified—at a time. The active control has a heavy outline and has sizing handles attached. Click anywhere on a control to make it active if it isn't already.

When a control is created, Visual Basic gives it a default name. This name includes the control's type and a sequentially assigned number. You can change control names in the Properties window to make them more mean-ingful, and you probably should do so as soon as they're created. This can eliminate problems and confusion later.

## Finding Controls in a Project

Whenever you add a new control to a project, it immediately appears in lists throughout the current form and items associated with it. For example, the control's name appears in the Object drop-down list at the very top of the Properties window. Its name also appears in the Object drop-down list at the top right of the Code window, across from the Proc: drop-down list. Figure 5.2 shows one of these drop-down lists.

**Figure 5.2**
The Object drop-down list in the Properties window, showing a control in this project.

Because control captions are generally different from the actual name of a control, it can be difficult to locate a particular control by name. You could just select each control in turn and access the Properties window to determine its name. Alternatively, to find a particular control on the current form:

1. Have the appropriate project open.

2. Choose Properties from the Visual Basic View menu, or press the F4 key.

   The Properties window appears.

3. Click the drop-down list at the top of the Properties window; click to select the control name.

4. Double-click the Properties window's control menu icon to close the window. The control remains selected on the current form.

## Removing a Control from a Form

If you accidentally add a control you don't need, or if you find a control you added previously doesn't suit you any longer, you easily can delete it from the project. Doing so is much easier than deleting a form from a project.

To remove a control from a project:

1. Display the form window.

2. Click to select the object you want to remove.

3. Press Del on your keyboard.

4. The control is removed from the project. Its name disappears from all drop-down lists.

**Note**   You also can use the Clipboard to temporarily or permanently remove controls. Click to select the control, and choose Cut from the Edit menu (or press Ctrl+X). The control is cut to the Clipboard. You then can paste it elsewhere—say onto another form—using the Edit Paste command (or press Ctrl+V).

# Control Types

There are several different types of controls, each meant for a specific purpose, and having different properties and behaviors. Figure 5.3 shows a few different controls on a form.

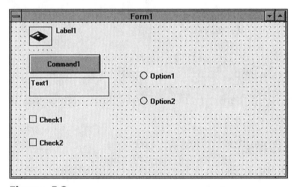

**Figure 5.3**
Several different examples of controls.

Some of the more important and commonly used controls include:

| Control | Function |
| --- | --- |
| Picture Box | Provides a frame for a graphic. User can click this control to perform an action |

| Control | Function |
|---|---|
| Label | Provides a text label for other items, including controls. User can click a label to perform an action |
| Text Box | Provides a place into which user may type text |
| Frame | Provides a structure in which other, like controls may be grouped |
| Command Button | Performs an action when a user clicks it |
| List Box | Provides a list of text choices |
| Horizontal or Vertical Scroll Bar | Provides a method for moving contents of a form window, to see things that cannot all be displayed at once. You must write program code to enable scroll bars |
| Common Dialog | Creates dialog boxes; requires the file CMDIALOG.VBX be loaded into the project using the Add File command |

# Adjusting Controls

Once you've added a control to a form, there are a number of things you can do to make it suit your purpose. You can change its size, position, and properties.

## Resizing

The simplest thing to do to a control is to change its size. A Visual Basic control has sizing handles that appear when the control is selected. You use the sizing handles to change a control's size. Figure 5.4 shows a control resizing operation in progress.

To change the size of a control, follow these steps:

1. Use the Project window to display the appropriate form, if it isn't already open and active. Click to select the control to resize.

2. Move the mouse pointer over the control's lower-right sizing handle. The pointer turns into a diagonal, double-headed arrow like that shown in Figure 5.4.

3. Click and drag the sizing handle in the appropriate direction: up and left to make the control smaller, down and right to make it larger.

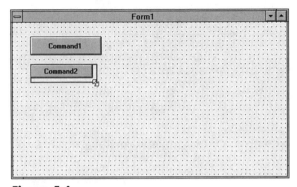

**Figure 5.4**
Changing the size of a control.

> 4. Release the mouse button when you've dragged the control to the desired size.

 **Tip** You don't have to use the control's lower-right sizing handle. Drag the control's bottom-center sizing handle to make the control taller or shorter; drag the control's right-center sizing handle to make it wider or narrower.

## Control Positioning

Another common thing to do to a control is to change its position. All you have to do is to drag the control where you want it. Figure 5.5 shows a control positioning operation in progress.

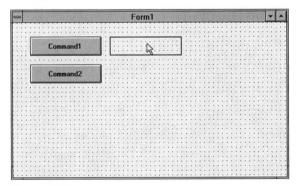

**Figure 5.5**
Repositioning a control.

To change the position of a control, perform these steps:

1. Use the Project window to display the appropriate form, if it isn't already open and active. Click to select the correct control on the form.

2. Move the mouse pointer over the control and press and hold the mouse button.

3. Drag the control to its new position.

4. Release the mouse button.

## Control Properties

As with forms, size and position are not the only qualities a control possesses. Controls also possess properties. You can view—and possibly change—these properties using the Properties window, as shown in Figure 5.6.

**Figure 5.6**
The Properties window, showing the current properties of Command1.

To view the properties for a given control, follow these steps:

1. Display the form whose properties you want to examine. Click to select the appropriate control.

2. Choose the Properties command from the Visual Basic Window menu, or press F4 on your keyboard.

   The Properties window appears, displaying the control's current property settings.

**Tip** You can enlarge the Properties window to view more properties at a time and to see each more fully. You can drag the scroll bar to view all the control's properties. Click the control menu icon to close the Property window.

As with forms, there are a number of control properties, some of which you might never use. Certain properties affect how controls appear, others how they behave.

**Note** Although it's appropriate to set certain control properties using the Properties window—such as a control's caption and color—other items should really be changed dynamically within the execution of your Visual Basic program. This is really what it's all about with both forms and controls. You'll learn more about this process in Lesson 7, "Manipulating Data: Expressions and Operations."

### List of Available Properties

You should know that all controls do not have the same properties. The properties listed in the following table are for the command button control.

Here's a list of some of the more important control properties:

| Control | Function |
| --- | --- |
| BackColor | Sets the control's background color, using the color palette |
| Caption | Sets the text to use within the control |
| Font | Sets the font name, style, and size to use in the control caption |
| Index | Creates control array. Specifies the current control's array number |
| MousePointer | Selects from among available mouse pointers to use when the pointer is over the control |
| Name | Sets the control's name |
| TabIndex | Sets where the control appears in tab order; this affects when or if the control is selected when the Tab key is pressed |
| TabStop | Sets whether to put the control into tab order |
| Visible | Sets whether the control can be seen and worked with |

**Note** Probably the best way to see what these various options do is to experiment with them in Visual Basic. Try changing property settings to see the effect this has. You needn't save your work.

### Setting the Properties

In terms of how you set them, control properties fall into two broad classes. There are some for which you enter a text item, and others for which you choose one item from an option list or a dialog box.

To determine what sort of property you're dealing with, check out the drop-down menu icon at the top of the Properties window, next to the box that shows the selected property's current setting. If you see a dimmed arrow there, the property is set by entering text. If the arrow isn't dimmed, you set the property with a drop-down list; click the arrow to see the list. If you see an ellipsis, the property is set with a dialog box.

### Using an Edit Box

To repeat, to determine whether a certain property is set by entering text, look at the drop-down menu icon next to the edit box. A dimmed arrow tells you that you must enter text to change the property.

To change a text item property, follow these steps:

1. Select the appropriate control and display the Properties window.

2. Click to select the name of the property you want to change.

3. Type in the new value for the property in the edit box at the top of the Properties window, below the drop-down list for object names.

4. Click the checkmark icon next to the edit box to save changes.

5. Double-click the Properties window's control menu icon to send it away, if desired.

### Using an Option List or Dialog Box

Rather than entering text, some control properties require you to make a choice from among available options. These options may be presented by way of an option list that drops down when you click a drop-down menu icon in the Properties window. Certain properties, such as the Picture property, require you to specify a file's location using a dialog box. These properties are labeled with an ellipsis icon. Figures 5.7 and 5.8 show both such alternatives.

**Figure 5.7**
Choosing a property setting from an option list.

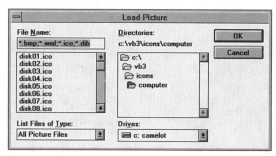

**Figure 5.8**
Choosing a property setting with a dialog box.

To change a property for which there is a choice, follow these steps:

1. Select the appropriate control and display the Properties window.

2. Click to select the name of the property you want to change.

3. Click the icon to the right of the edit box.

4. In an option list, click the name of the choice you want; then click OK.

   In a dialog box, use the Drive, Directory, and File lists to navigate to where the file you want to use (such as a bitmap or icon file) is located, and click to select its name; then click OK.

5. Double-click the Properties window's control menu icon to close it, if desired.

**Note** For a property set with the Open File dialog box: If you set the property at design time, as described previously, a copy of the item is taken into your program; you don't need the original. If, on the other hand, your program sets the property at run time, the original item is not taken into your Visual Basic project; it remains in its previous location on your hard disk. If the original item is changed outside of your project, you'll see the change in your project the next time you open it. If you move the item, however, Visual Basic won't be able to find it, and will tell you so, in an error message, when your program runs.

# Defining Procedures for a Control

A control's procedures define what the program will do when various events happen to the control. Recall that an event is generated when the user performs some particular action on a control, such as clicking the mouse. (It's possible to write a procedure—a list of program steps to perform—for every action a user might be expected to engage in with that control.

The following is a summary of some of the more important events associated with controls:

| Control | Action |
| --- | --- |
| Click | User clicks control |
| DoubleClick | User double-clicks control |
| KeyPress | User presses key on keyboard with control active |
| MouseDown | User presses mouse button with pointer over control |
| MouseUp | User releases mouse button with pointer over control |

You define event procedures for a control using the Visual Basic Code window. Figure 5.9 shows the Code window for the current control. Note in particular the Proc: drop-down list for events; use this to create a particular event procedure—by choosing from this list the event you want to define.

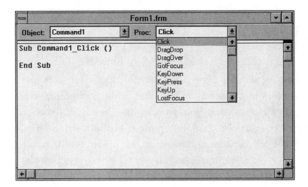

**Figure 5.9**
The Code window for Command1, opened, with the Proc list dropped down.

**Note** You should note the way Visual Basic refers to defined event procedures. A procedure always has a name. For an event procedure, this name includes the object type to which it belongs, with the event for which it's defined as a suffix.

To define a control procedure for a specific event, follow these steps:

1. Display the appropriate form, and double-click the control whose procedures you want to define.

   The Code window appears.

2. Choose the appropriate event from the Proc: drop-down list. Opening and closing statements for the procedure appear in the Code window, with the text insertion point appearing on a blank line between them.

3. Type the necessary Visual Basic program code to define the procedure.

4. Double-click the Code window's control menu icon to close the window.

**Note** Save your work often! Use the File menu's Save Project command to save changes to all parts of the current project, or Save File to save changes only to the active part. When you save changes to a form, all its controls are saved.

# Review

In this lesson, you learned the following:

☐ You add new controls to an application using the toolbox.

☐ You remove a control from a project using the Del key.

☐ You can resize or reposition a control by using its grow boxes and by dragging the entire control, respectively.

☐ Controls, just like forms, have a number of properties associated with them; these properties determine how the controls look and behave. You can change control properties using the Properties window, which you access with the Properties command in the Visual Basic Window menu (or by pressing F4). Control properties also can be set within procedures as part of program execution.

☐ A control has Visual Basic language procedures for any event that a user may perform on it. Event procedures are defined using the Code window, which can be accessed by way of a button on the Project window, by choosing Code from the View menu, by double-clicking the object for which you want to define a procedure, or by pressing the F7 key.

Now you should be ready for the quiz.

## Lesson 6

# About Variables

## Overview

Programs are all about performing operations on data. A moment's reflection will reveal the need for a place to hold data while the work is in progress. Moreover, as certain operations are apt to be repeated many times (or else what's the point of having a computer program do the work?), these storage places ought to be capable of handling different items of data at different times. In Visual Basic, as in all other programming languages, these needs are met by *variables*.

This lesson covers the following points regarding variables:

- ☐ What variables are, and how they're created
- ☐ Variables for different types of data
- ☐ Single variables that handle many items of data
- ☐ Restricting variables for use in specific places within an application program
- ☐ Having variables and their contents persist throughout a program

## Introducing Variables

Before using variables in your programs, you need to understand more about their purpose and how they're created. Figure 6.1 shows several variables being created within a Visual Basic program.

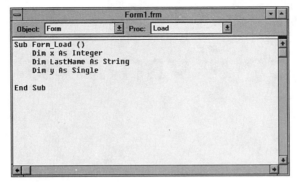

**Figure 6.1**
Creating variables *x*, *LastName*, and *y*.

## The Purpose of Variables

The concept of a computer program variable is borrowed from algebra. (And you thought you'd never use it after you got out of school.) You may have encountered variables in statements like

$$y=x^2 + 2x + 1$$

which describes a parabola. In Visual Basic, as in algebra, a *variable* is a named entity that represents some unknown value. Thus, a variable has both a name and contents. In math, the whole problem is to determine a variable's contents under given conditions, such as determining the value of *y* above when *x* is equal to 2. (It happens to be 9.) In programming, the point of a variable is to provide a placeholder within a program for data that may change.

Some things to keep in mind about variable names:

- ☐ Names must begin with a letter (a-z, lower- or uppercase)

- ☐ Names can't contain a period

- ☐ Names must be unique; no variables with the same name in the same location (for example, within a procedure)

- ☐ Names can contain up to 255 characters

## How Variables Are Created

As a default, you can have Visual Basic create a variable simply by using its name within a statement. Figure 6.2 shows a variable being declared in just such a context. We call this kind of variable creation *implicit declaration*.

```
┌─────────────────────────────────────────────┐
│ ⊟              Form1.frm               ▼ ▲  │
├─────────────────────────────────────────────┤
│ Object: Form        ▼   Proc: Load        ▼ │
├─────────────────────────────────────────────┤
│ Sub Form_Load ()                          ↑ │
│ Dim Subtotal                                │
│ Dim MarkDown                                │
│ Dim MyCut                                   │
│                                             │
│ Subtotal = 1448                             │
│ MarkDown = .2                               │
│ Total = Subtotal - (Subtotal * MarkDown)    │
│ MyCut = Totl * .5                           │
│                                             │
│ End Sub                                     │
│ |                                         ↓ │
├─────────────────────────────────────────────┤
│ ←  ←                                    →   │
└─────────────────────────────────────────────┘
```

**Figure 6.2**
Implicitly declaring the variable Total.

You can encounter problems with variables created "on the fly" through implicit declaration. The most obvious are typographical errors. If you type both **Total** and **Totl**, Visual Basic creates two variables; it doesn't know you've simply mistyped the variable name in the second case. This leads to an error when the program is run.

A better way to create variables is to declare them explicitly. To do so, you insert the appropriate statement before any other programming code that appears in the part of your program you're working on. (This part is called a *module*; there is always at least one form module associated with each form, and perhaps one or more standard modules that contain general procedures applying to the whole program.) Figure 6.1 showed three variables being declared explicitly within the form module for Form1.

**Note** Declaring variables explicitly doesn't resolve the problem with mistyping variable names. You have to tell Visual Basic not to allow variables to be defined implicitly. To do this, insert the statement:

```
Option Explicit
```

at the beginning of each module (form or standard) in your program. This option also can be set for the entire program; see Lesson 8, "Managing Projects."

You can declare a variable within the procedure in which it's used with the Dim statement. Figure 6.3 shows the variable *Total* being declared in this way.

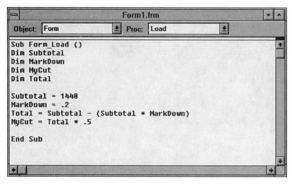

```
Sub Form_Load ()
Dim Subtotal
Dim MarkDown
Dim MyCut
Dim Total

Subtotal = 1448
MarkDown = .2
Total = Subtotal - (Subtotal * MarkDown)
MyCut = Total * .5

End Sub
```

**Figure 6.3**
Explicitly declaring the variable *Total*.

The following points are important when it comes to declaring variables explicitly:

- [ ] A variable declared with the Dim statement within a procedure will work only within that procedure. A variable declared with the same name in a different procedure will be, in effect, a different variable with different contents.

- [ ] A variable declared with Dim within a procedure exists only while the procedure is running. The variable and its contents "disappear" at the end of the procedure.

- [ ] It is possible to create a variable to be used outside a single procedure and to stay in existence throughout a program's execution. (These techniques are explained later in this lesson.)

# Variables for Different Purposes

Although variables may seem like a "one-size-fits-all" topic, there are a number of ways to create variables to fit more specific data-storage needs. These methods include choosing the specific type of data a variable can support, and determining the number of items that can fit within it.

## Fundamental Data Types

The standard kind of Visual Basic variable, called a variant, is meant as a sort of "catch-all" variable that can handle different sorts of data. For certain purposes, however, it may be more efficient to explicitly define a variable as supporting one kind of data—numeric, character, monetary figures, and so on—and one kind only. Visual Basic supports several specific variable types, all declared using the As keyword. Figure 6.1 showed three variables being declared with this keyword.

### Variant

*Variant* is the Visual Basic default variable type. It can handle both numeric and character data—whatever you put into it. Although you can explicitly declare a variable of type "variant" using the As keyword, you get the same result by omitting the keyword all together, as in this following example:

```
Dim Holder
Dim Place As Variant
```

In this example, both *Holder* and *Place* are variables of type "variant."

Some things to know about variant variables:

- ☐ A variant variable that has not yet been used to store data has the value Empty. This value is treated as either the number 0, or as a zero-length string " ", depending on the context.

- ☐ A variant can be assigned the value "Null"—to indicate missing information, for example. The result of any numeric or character operation involving Null is always Null.

- ☐ Using a variant in numeric and character operations can cause unexpected results if the contents of the variables involved are of different types. In particular, it is best to use the "&" operator for combining strings (concatenating) instead of "+".

### Whole Number Variables: Integer and Long

A variant variable is not an efficient choice if what you really want to store is whole-number data. In this case, you should create variables of types Integer and Long. The following two lines of code create an integer and a long integer variable, respectively.

```
Dim X As Integer
Dim Y As Long
```

Integer variables can store numbers from –32,768 to 32,767. Long variables can store numbers from –2,147,483,648 to 2,147,483,647. If you want to store numbers outside this range or that have fractional parts, you need to use either Single or Double type variables.

### Real Number Variables: Single and Double

Visual Basic has variables types Single and Double for storing real numbers—that is, numbers that may have fractional parts. The following two lines of code create a single-precision floating point variable named *Coefficient* and a double-precision floating point variable named *VerySmallNumber*.

```
Dim Coefficient As Single
Dim VerySmallNumber As Double
```

The approximate range for Single variables is $-3.4 \times 10^{45}$ to $3.4 \times 10^{38}$. The range for Double variables is $-1.8 \times 10^{308}$ to $1.8 \times 10^{308}$. (Note that the total number of subatomic particles in the known universe is thought to be less than $1 \times 10^{90}$.)

### Currency

What if you want to work with monetary values—dollars and cents? Integers won't do, because there's no space for cents. Single and Double variables seem like overkill. What's more, Single and Double variables can be subject to rounding-off errors when used in interest and other calculations. Fortunately, Visual Basic provides a numeric data type that surmounts these problems. The following line of code creates a currency variable.

```
Dim Salary As Currency
```

The Currency variable type supports values from –922,337,203,685,477.5808 to 922,337,203,685,477.5807. Such numbers ought to support the value of the national debt into the first part of the next century. Note that four places to the right of the decimal are supported; this allows calculations in *Mils*. A mil is 1/1000th of a dollar.

### String

So much for numeric data. Visual Basic also has a data type for variables meant to include only *character data*, also called *alphanumeric data*. These are data such as words and figures presented for their literal, rather than their numeric, content. The following line of code creates a character, or *string* variable.

```
Dim Name As String
```

x

String variables can be of variable length—as in the previous declaration—or they can support a fixed length. To create a String variable with a fixed length, include that length within parentheses after the variable's name.

```
Dim SerialNumber As String(10)
```

A variable-length string may be slightly less efficient in some cases. One string variable can hold up to about 65,000 characters on all systems, and up to $2 \times 10^{32}$ characters on 32-bit systems such as Windows NT.

### About Logical Values

For certain calculations involving logical operations, you need variables that contain neither numeric or character data. Many other programming languages offer logical variables (often named *Boolean variables*, after George Boole, who's credited with inventing this sort of logic). Visual Basic does not offer this data type at this writing. You can, however, store logical values True and False in Variant type variables

```
Dim LikesGreenEggs As Variant
```

When used in logical operations, a Variant type variable that hasn't yet been assigned a value is interpreted as having the logical value False.

**Note**  The number 0, described in an early section of this lesson as being one interpretation of the contents of an Empty Variant variable, is a synonym for False.

### Constants

In certain cases, you should give an unchanging value a name, just as a variable has. Such an entity is called a *constant*. You may be familiar with constants from mathematics and physics: pi and Avogadro's number are both constants. You declare constants using the Const keyword; at the same time, you must assign the constant's value. The two lines of code shown below show two constants being created and assigned values.

```
Public Const Pi = 3.1415928
Const InflationRate = 3
```

The changeable parts of this expression include the constant's name, whether to make it public or private, and its precise value. After a constant is declared, it is referred to by name. Here, the variable *CircleArea* is being set to the product of the constant Pi multiplied by the value of a variable named Radius after Radius is squared.

```
CircleArea=Pi*Radius^2
```

## Arrays: Many Variables with One Name

Up to this point, we've considered variables that hold but a single value, although that value can be any of several different types. In some cases, though, it's convenient to group several values under a single heading, referring to them by their position number or numbers within the group.

Real life is full of things that look and act like multiple-value variables. Think of a checkerboard, for example. You can specify any square on a checkerboard by indicating which row and column it's in. In this way, each square on the board can be uniquely identified without having to individually name every square.

As in most programming languages, you create multiple-value variables in Visual Basic using *arrays*. The following line of code creates a 10-member array.

```
Redim TestScores(9) As Integer
```

The previous statement creates the array named TestScores. This array contains 10 (Visual Basic starts counting with 0) integer values. The number after the array name is called the *index*, which you use to refer to a specific item, or element, within the array. For example,

```
TestScores(2) = 90
```

assigns the value "90" to the third element in the array. It's possible to have a variable or an expression to refer to which element to use, as in:

```
TestScores(x) = 90
```

In this case, the element assigned "90" depends on the contents of $x$; if $x$ contains 3, then the fourth element receives the indicated value. Using variables as indexes is where you harness the real power of arrays. As you'll see in Lesson 9, "Making Decisions," you can have just three statements perform an operation on every element in an array, no matter how big. You just have to use the appropriate variable name to reference items in the array.

As with our checkerboard example, an array may have more than one index; such an array is called a *multidimensional array*.

```
Redim TestScores(9,2) As Integer
```

In this example, the array TestScores has 30 values. You could think of them as arranged in a table, with ten rows (remember, Visual Basic counts 0 through 9) and three columns (0 through 2). Such an array might store scores for ten students on three separate exams. The specific item

```
TestScores(3,1)
```

would then refer to the fourth student's score on the second test, while

```
TestScores(0,0)
```

refers to the first student's score on the first test.

# A Variable's Field of Action

A single variable isn't necessarily supported everywhere in your application unless you explicitly declare it so when creating it. What's more, the variable and its contents may be only temporary. There are ways to adjust both these parameters—the variable's range of action and its lifetime—to suit your needs.

## Scopes for Variables

All Visual Basic variables possess an important quality called *scope*, which is the extent within the program to which the variable may be referred. There is an opposition between variables that are *local* in scope, meaning they're available only with the procedure or module in which they were declared, and variables that are *global*, meaning they're available to all procedures or modules.

### Local

Variables declared with the Dim keyword are available only within the procedure or module in which they were declared. Depending on where they're declared, however, local variables declared with Dim actually can have different scopes. In Figure 6.4, the variable *Total1* is local to the Form1 module as a whole, the variable *Total2* is local to the Command1_Click procedure. *Total1* is available to every procedure in Form1; *Total2* is available only within the Command1_Click procedure.

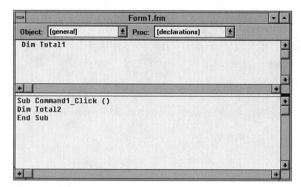

**Figure 6.4**
Two local variables, each with a different scope.

Keep these ideas in mind when creating variables for local use:

☐ A variable created within a procedure is local to that procedure; you cannot access its contents outside that procedure. Attempting to do so in another procedure simply creates a new variable, probably with no contents.

☐ A variable created at the head of a module, in its declarations section as shown in Figure 6.4, is local to that module, but it is available to all procedures within that module.

☐ You cannot declare a global variable within a procedure. If you could, you'd expect this to make the variable available to all procedures in the module. In fact, you do this by declaring the global variables in the declarations section of a code module.

### Global

It may be that you want certain variables to be available within all modules in a program. You can do so using the Global keyword. This keyword can be used only in the declarations part of a module, outside of any and all procedures. Figure 6.5 shows variables being declared publicly.

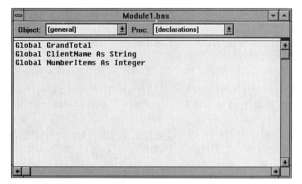

**Figure 6.5**
Three global variables.

## Variable Lifetime: Dynamic versus Static

As a rule, a local variable can survive only as long as the procedure or module that it's in is executing. Afterward, it (and its contents) disappears from computer memory. If your program runs the procedure again, the variable is created again, but its previous contents will not have been preserved. You can think of such a variable as being *dynamic* in nature. You can, however, cause a variable to remain in memory by declaring it with the Static keyword. The following line of code creates a static variable named *Accumulator*.

```
Static Accumulator As Integer
```

Some points about static variables:

- [ ] Static applies only to local variables; a global variable is, in a sense, already static because it is available in all modules and procedures.

- [ ] A static local variable cannot be changed by another procedure.

- [ ] All variables within a procedure can be made implicitly static by using the Static keyword before the procedure name, as in:

```
Static Sub MyProcedure()
```

# Review

In this lesson, you learned the following:

☐ Variables are named places in which you store data. You create them by declaring them in a line of code—either implicitly by using them, or explicitly by using a `Dim` or other such statement.

☐ There are a number of variable types for storing different kinds of data, including integers, real numbers, characters, and varying data.

☐ It is possible to create an array variable, which has one name but places for multiple values. The individual values in an array are referenced by indexes. Array variables can have multiple indexes (be multi-dimensional).

☐ Private variables are local to the procedure or module in which they were created. Using the Dim or Static keywords in a declaration makes a variable local. Global variables are available throughout a program. Using the Global keyword as part of a variable's declaration makes it global. This keyword cannot be used within a procedure.

☐ A local variable can be made to persist throughout a program's execution using the Static keyword. Such a variable's contents do not disappear when the defining procedure quits running, although its contents cannot be accessed or changed by other procedures.

Now you should be ready for the quiz.

## Lesson 7

# Manipulating Data: Expressions and Operations

## Overview

Computer programs are all about manipulating data: adding up columns of financial figures in a spreadsheet, applying formatting to text in a word processor, and storing names and addresses in a database are but a few examples. Clearly, there's a way to tell a computer what to do with certain data, and how to do it. In fact, these capabilities lie at the very core of any programming language, such as Visual Basic. This lesson introduces you to the data manipulation techniques native to the BASIC part of the Visual Basic programming environment, which we first talked about in Lesson 1, "Introducing Visual Basic and the CD Tutor."

This lesson covers the following points regarding the BASIC part of Visual Basic and its fundamentals:

- ☐ How you organize instructions in Visual Basic

- ☐ The different mathematical operations available, such as multiplication and addition

- ☐ Operations to use on character strings, such as combining two strings into one

- ☐ Operations to perform logical evaluations, such as comparing two variables to find out which is larger

- ☐ How to move results into storage

# About Expressions and Statements

You'll recall from earlier lessons that the work of a Visual Basic application program is accomplished in procedures. A procedure is like a recipe, telling you—step-by-step—how to accomplish a usually small task. Each step in a procedure corresponds to a single *statement* in the Visual Basic programming language. A statement, in turn, can have one or more *expressions*. Figure 7.1 shows five statements in the Visual Basic code window. The fourth statement contains a mathematical expression.

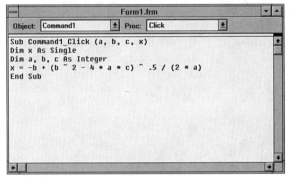

```
Form1.frm
Object: Command1        Proc: Click

Sub Command1_Click (a, b, c, x)
Dim x As Single
Dim a, b, c As Integer
x = -b + (b ^ 2 - 4 * a * c) ^ .5 / (2 * a)
End Sub
```

**Figure 7.1**
The five Visual Basic statements shown begin a procedure, create four variables in two statements, define a mathematical expression, and end the procedure.

## Parts of a Statement

Looking at Figure 7.1, you can get an idea of what goes in a typical Visual Basic statement. A statement generally includes one or more *keywords* or *symbols*. A keyword is a single word that signifies a specific action in Visual Basic. For example, the keyword Sub identifies a procedure. The symbol = (read as "becomes" rather than "equals") identifies a statement that puts the value to the right of the symbol in the place specified on the left. Another important part of a Visual Basic statement is its expressions, such as the one on the right of the equal sign in the fourth statement shown in Figure 7.1.

## About Expressions

The concept of an expression, like that of a variable, is borrowed from algebra. An *expression* is a group of symbols representing a specific value. We say that the expression *evaluates* to the value in question. In the example in

Figure 7.1, the expression shown in the fourth statement evaluates to one of the roots of a quadratic equation. The exact value of the expression depends, of course, on the values contained in the variables a, b, and c.

An expression always evaluates to a single value. Again, the exact value depends on the contents of any variables in the expression. The type of data contained in these variables is also critical to the evaluation of an expression. In general, there are three types of expressions:

☐ A *numerical expression* resulting in a number (integer, real, or currency)

☐ A *text expression* resulting in a character string

☐ A *logical expression* resulting in either True or False

Figure 7.2 shows examples of all three expression types.

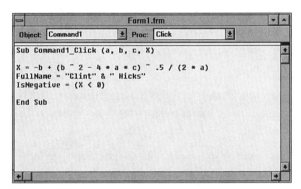

**Figure 7.2**
The three central statements in this figure each show a different type of Visual Basic expression.

## Types of Statements

Just as there are types of expressions, there also are types of statements. Expressions can form part of any of these statement types. Figure 7.3 shows examples of the three main statement types.

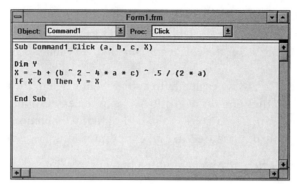

**Figure 7.3**
A variable declaration statement, an assignment statement, and a program control statement.

The three fundamental types of Visual Basic statements are:

- ☐ *Variable Declaration Statements.* We talked about these statements in Lesson 6, "About Variables." A variable declaration statement creates one or more variables, with specified names, of a given variable type and scope.

- ☐ *Assignment Statements.* These statements move data into (assign data to) variables, including object properties. You can distinguished them by the presence of the equal sign (=).

- ☐ *Program Control Statements.* These statements perform a variety of tasks, such as declaring procedures and controlling the order in which a program's statements execute. You'll find out more about statement execution in Lesson 9, "Making Decisions."

The rest of this lesson covers various forms of assignment statements and the different kinds of expressions (with their associated operations) that go into them.

## Assignment Statements

You know that assignment statements move data from one place to another. A simple assignment statement might place constant data in a variable, such as

```
LastName = "Hicks"
```

but a more useful version of an assignment statement evaluates an expression, and puts it in the variable, as in

```
FuturePopulation = PresentPopulation * (e ^ (Rate * Time))
```

Notice that an assignment statement moves data from right to left: it evaluates the expression to the right of the equal sign, and that value moves to the variable on the left of the equal sign. In a sense, an assignment statement does set the two items equal, although they probably weren't prior to the statement's execution.

### Getting Data into Variables

To move the value of an expression into a variable, you only need to specify the variable, followed by an equal sign, and then the relevant expression. The relevant expression can be mathematical, a character string, or logical—depending on the type of data you're manipulating. Figure 7.4 shows three variable assignment statements, each using a different kind of data.

**Figure 7.4**
Three assignment statements that work with character, logical, and numeric data, respectively.

Here are some things to keep in mind about variable assignment statements:

☐ Generally, you can't mix data types in an expression. In some cases, Visual Basic tries to perform the indicated operation (adding the value of an integer variable to the value of a character string variable, for example) but the results are not what you expect. In other cases, Visual Basic generates a Type Mismatch error and your program ceases to run.

☐ Attempting to assign data of one type to a variable of another type also results in a `Type Mismatch` error.

☐ When you assign a new value to a variable, it overrides the previous contents. Thus, whatever the variable *x* contained before, the statement:

x=0

destroys the former contents of *x* and replaces them with 0.

**Note**  When first declared, a variable has no value. Numeric variables are set to 0, character variables set to a zero-length string, and variant variables are set to Null. If this causes a problem in your program, you need to quickly use an assignment statement to give your variable a more acceptable value.

### Getting Data into Object Properties

Just as you can move data from an expression into a variable, you also can use assignment statements to set object properties. Figure 7.5 shows three object properties being assigned new values.

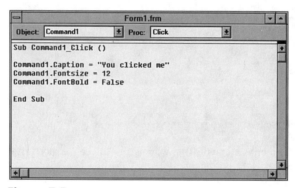

**Figure 7.5**
Assigning values to the `Caption`, `FontSize`, and `FontBold` properties of the command button `Command1`.

As you can see, assigning new values to object properties is slightly more involved than assigning data to variables. For one thing, specifying the property to change involves naming the object and property, and perhaps even the module to which the object belongs.

**Referencing Object Properties**  To assign a value to an object property, you must reference it completely. To reference a property, use the property's name, the name of the object whose property you're changing, and possibly the form or module to which the object belongs. Each of these items is separated by a period, as in:

```
Form1.Command1.Caption = "Click Me"
```

In this example, Form1 refers to the form on which the object Command1 is found. Caption is the name of the property being changed. This assignment statement changes the caption of the button named Command1 on Form1 to read Click Me.

Omit the form or module if you're referencing a control in the current form. For instance, if you have a click procedure associated with a command button on Form1 that changes a label caption on the same form, you can omit the Form1 designation and use something like:

```
Label1.Caption = "You clicked the button"
```

**About Object Values**  For some object properties, you even can omit the property name in an assignment statement. You see, each object has a *value;* this is the most important property, or most commonly used of all the properties possessed by the object. Figure 7.6 shows the results of using an object's value directly in an assignment statement.

**Figure 7.6**
This statement assigns data to a label's value, which is the Caption property.

The following table summarizes which property is considered the value of the most important control objects:

| Control | Value Property |
| --- | --- |
| Check box | Value |
| Command button | Value |
| Common dialog box | Action |
| Directory list box | Path |
| Drive list box | Drive |
| File list box | FileName |
| Frame | Caption |
| Horizontal scroll bar | Value |
| Image | Picture |
| Label | Caption |
| Line | Visible |
| List box | Text |
| Menu | Enabled |
| Option button | Value |
| Picture box | Picture |
| Shape | Shape |
| Text box | Text |
| Timer | Enabled |
| Vertical scroll bar | Value |

For any control listed above, you can omit the name of the value property whenever you're assigning data to that property.

# About Operations

To this point, you've seen how to move data from an expression into a variable or object property. However, we haven't looked very closely inside expressions. It's time to remedy that.

Remember that an expression is a group of symbols that evaluates to a particular result; this result can be a number, a character string, or a logical value (True or False). The symbols we've been referring to can be the names of variables and the values of constants, and also can tell the computer what to do with them. These symbols are called *operators;* the operations they perform fall into the same broad categories as the expressions in which they're found: mathematical, string, and logical.

## Mathematical Operations

The mathematical operators available in Visual Basic are familiar from everyday arithmetic. Figure 7.7 shows three assignment statements containing mathematical operations.

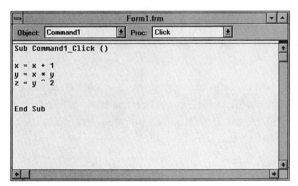

**Figure 7.7**
The three central statements show the mathematical operations of addition, multiplication, and exponentiation, respectively.

The following table is a list of the mathematical operators available in Visual Basic:

| Symbol | Meaning |
|---|---|
| + | Add two numbers |
| − | Subtract two numbers |
| * | Multiply two numbers<br>You cannot omit the multiplication sign as you can in algebra; a * (b + c) is not the same thing as a(b + c). In the latter case, Visual Basic thinks you're referring to an array variable |
| / | Divide first number by second, yield real result |
| \ | Divide first number by second, yield integer result (fractional portion of answer is rounded to nearest integer) |
| MOD | Perform modular arithmetic; divide first number evenly by second, discard result and retain remainder (7 MOD 3 equals 1. 8 MOD 2 equals 0.) |
| ^ | Raise first number to power of the second. 7 ^ 3 is seven cubed, or 343. You use fractional values to obtain roots; 343 ^ (1/3) equals 7 |

Obviously, you can combine operators to create complex expressions. Parentheses are useful in such cases because they keep parts of an expression separate, and control how it's evaluated. For example, the following two expressions aren't the same:

2 + 3 * 4

(2 + 3) * 4

The former evaluates to 14, the latter evaluates to 20. That's because multiplication precedes addition whenever an expression is evaluated. We'll have more to say on the order of evaluation in the section "Order of Operations," later in this chapter.

## String Operations

String operators apply to character string data; there are far fewer of these than there are mathematical operators. Most operations on strings, in fact, are performed by special procedures called string functions. We'll talk about such functions in Lesson 14, "Methods, Procedures, and Functions." Figure 7.8 shows a few string operations that we will talk about here.

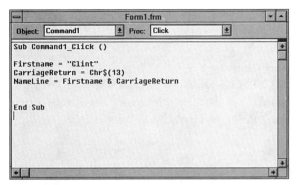

**Figure 7.8**
The three string operations shown above create a literal string 'Clint,' use the Chr$ function to convert a number value to its ANSI character equivalent, and concatenate the contents of two variables.

The following is a list of some string operations available in Visual Basic.

| Symbol | Meaning |
| --- | --- |
| + | Concatenate two strings; that is, put the first string together with the second string to yield a third string. Note that using this operator is ambiguous, because it can also mean addition. |
| & | Another version of concatenation, but forces concatenation if one part of the expression is numeric. It's better to use this operator symbol. |
| " " | Quote the enclosed material. You use this operator to get a particular character string into a string variable or expression. Enclose the desired data (sometimes called a string constant) in quotes. To embed quotes in a string, use two quotes in succession. |
| Chr$(*numeric expression*) | This is really a string function, but it is very useful to learn it right away. It converts the numeric expression in parentheses into its ANSI character equivalent. ANSI is a standard that associates integer values from 0 to 255 with specific characters and, perhaps more importantly, with control codes such as carriage returns. You can use this function to get a carriage return (Chr$(13)), or any other ANSI character, into a string. |

## Logical Operations

You use logical operators to test expressions and determine whether they meet specified conditions. There are additional logical operators to modify the results of such a test, or to combine the results of two or more tests. The former logical operators are called comparison operators; we can refer to the latter as propositional operators.

### Comparison Operators

You use this set of operators to compare two variables or expressions (or one of each) to see if the specified criterion is met. Figure 7.9 shows three expressions containing comparison operators.

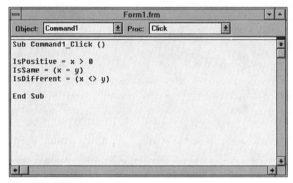

**Figure 7.9**
The three comparison operations shown here are "greater than," "equals," and "not equal to."

 Comparison operators include the following:

| Format | Operation | Meaning |
| --- | --- | --- |
| x<y | Less than | Compare two expressions: true if the first is less than the second, false otherwise |
| x>y | Greater than | Compare two expressions: true if the first is greater than the second, false otherwise |
| x=y | Equals | Compare two expressions: true if the first is the same as the second, false otherwise |
| x<>y | Not equal | Compare two expressions: true if the first is not the same as the second, false otherwise |
| x<=y | Less than or equal to | Compare two expressions: true if the first is less than or equal to the second, false otherwise |
| x>=y | Greater than or equal to | Compare two expressions: true if the first is greater than or equal to the second, false otherwise |

As with mathematical and string operators, you can use parentheses to group parts of a comparison expression.

### Propositional Operators

You use propositional operators to combine the results of two or more tests created with comparison operators. In this way, complex conditions can be evaluated. Figure 7.10 shows three such expressions.

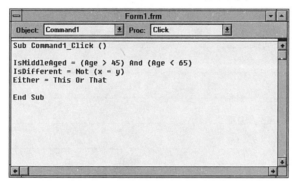

**Figure 7.10**
The middle three statements shown here feature the propositional operators And, Not, and Or.

Propositional operators include the following:

| Operation Format | Meaning |
| --- | --- |
| x And y | Evaluates to true if both expressions are true; false otherwise |
| x Or y | Evaluates to true if either or both expressions are true; it's false if both are false |
| x Xor y | Also known as "exclusive or." Evaluates to true if one expression or the other is true, but false if both are true or both are false |
| Not x | Negates the expression following it. Not False is the same as True |

## Order of Operations

You can create very complex expressions that are pretty much only limited by the amount of memory you have. The results of such a long expression, however, might not be what you expect. Visual Basic does not simply evaluate an expression from left to right, performing each operation as it goes. Rather, different operations are performed at different times according to a pre-defined set of rules, called the order of operations. This is yet another concept borrowed from algebra.

The following table shows the order in which operations are evaluated in Visual Basic.

| Operation | Symbol |
| --- | --- |
| Exponentiation | ^ |
| Equality | = |
| Negation | NOT |
| Negative | – |
| Inequality | <> |
| Logical addition | AND |
| Multiplication and Division | * and / |
| Less than | < |
| Logical multiplication | OR |
| Integer division | \ |
| Greater than | > |
| Exclusive or | XOR |
| Modular arithmetic | MOD |
| Less than or equal to | <= |
| Addition and Subtraction | + and – |
| Greater than or equal to | >= |
| Concatenation | & |

# Review

In this lesson, you learned the following:

☐ Visual Basic instructions are organized into statements.

☐ A statement may include one or more expressions, which are groups of symbols that evaluate to a specific result.

☐ Assignment statements, using the equal sign, are used to move data from an expression into a variable. They also may be used to change object properties.

☐ You use the name of the object and the property, separated by periods, to reference an object's properties. You also must include the name of the form or module first, if the object being referenced is outside the current form or module. You can omit the property name if it is the object's value—considered to be its most important property. Each object has a specific value.

☐ You use mathematical operators to perform arithmetic calculations. They include the standard symbols from arithmetic.

☐ String operators perform manipulations on character data. The most important of these is the concatenation operator, used to combine strings.

☐ Logical operations test conditions and yield true or false results. You can divide these operations into comparison operators that compare two expressions to see whether a given condition is met, and propositional operators, that are used to combine and modify the results of two or more comparisons.

☐ In a mixed expression involving several different operators, Visual Basic evaluates the expression in a strictly defined order.

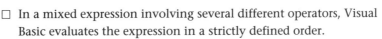

**Quiz**    Now you should be ready for the quiz.

# Managing Projects

## Overview

As we've introduced a large number of elements that go into a Visual Basic application program, it should be apparent to you that more needs to be said about how to keep track of them all. This is also a good time to talk about some overall Visual Basic options that determine how individual projects—and the program as a whole—behave in the design environment.

In this lesson, we'll cover these points:

☐ The parts of a Visual Basic project

☐ How to save a project or the parts thereof

☐ How to set options to control how Visual Basic behaves, and how it treats a particular project

## How Visual Basic Saves Your Work

Unlike some applications, the word processor Microsoft Word for example, Visual Basic doesn't preserve all the parts of a project in a single file. Instead, a project generally consists of a collection of files, including a sort of "master file" that refers to all the other files. Figure 8.1 shows the Visual Basic Project window with three of the files that a typical project might include. You can tell the file's type by the icon to the left of its name in the Project window.

**Figure 8.1**
Three parts of a Visual Basic application: a form module,
a standard module, and a custom control file.

## Project Parts

A Visual Basic project consists of one or more of the following files:

| Files | Purpose |
| --- | --- |
| Form modules | Contain information about the form's properties, controls, and procedures. Reside in a file with the extension .FRM. At least one form module is required |
| Custom controls | Enable you to incorporate extra control objects into your projects. Microsoft provides a number of these; you also can acquire custom controls from third-party developers. Control files have a .VBX extension |
| Standard modules | Contain general procedures and variable declarations. They bear the .BAS extension |

Visual Basic applications also support other parts, such as resource files and insertable objects. The former is beyond the scope of this book; the latter will be handled in Lesson 18, "Communicating with Other Programs."

### The MAK File

At the top of it all is the .MAK file. This file contains references to all the other parts of a project. Figure 8.2 shows the contents of a typical .MAK file.

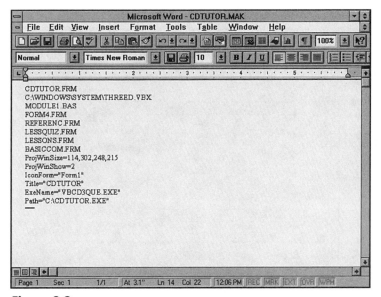

**Figure 8.2**
Contents of a .MAK file, viewed in a text editor.

.MAK files can include, among other things:

☐ Names of all forms and modules in the project, including which is the startup form

☐ Custom controls used by the project

☐ Initial size and position of the Project window

☐ Project file name

☐ Executable file name

# Saving Your Work

Before you can view a .MAK file for your own project, you have to save your work. Doing so creates the .MAK file and the component files to which it refers. It's also possible to save an existing project using another name—this creates a new .MAK file, which is a clone of the original project.

Introductory Topics

### The Save Project Command

You save a project using, appropriately enough, the Save Project command from the Visual Basic File menu. The first time you do this in a project, a dialog box appears (see fig. 8.3).

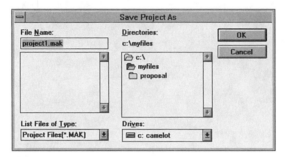

**Figure 8.3**
The Save Project As dialog box.

Take the following steps to save a project:

1. Choose Save Project from the Visual Basic File menu.

2a. *If nothing has been saved before*, the Save File As dialog box appears for each module (form and standard module) in the project. Type a name and select a location for each file, and then click OK. Proceed to 2b.

2b. *If files have been saved*, the Save Project As dialog box appears. Type a name for the new project, select a location, and then click OK.

    Recall that file names are limited to eight letters, plus a three-letter extension. Extensions for project file names are already determined.

Once a project has been saved for the first time, you can save any and all changes to it at any time by choosing Save Project again.

Use the Open Project command in the File menu to open an existing project. Only one project can be open at a time.

### Saving a Copy of a Project

If you want, you can save a copy of a project to another name or location. You then can make changes to the copy without altering the original project. Use the Save Project As command in the Visual Basic File menu. The dialog box appears exactly the same as that shown previously in Figure 8.3.

**Note** Keep in mind that any changes you make and save to the component files—forms and the like—in the new project will be reflected in the old project. If you want to preserve the original components while making alterations to suit the new project, you need to create copies of the components with the Save File As command; see the "Save File As" section later in this lesson.

# Preserving a Work in Progress

As work continues in a project, you'll want to save changes to individual project parts. Like with the project as a whole, you also can choose to save components under a new name. This enables you to make changes to a copy without affecting the original.

## Save File

When you choose the Save File command from the Visual Basic File menu, the active component (form or module) is saved to your hard disk. The first time you choose this command for a particular module, a dialog box like that shown in Figure 8.4 appears.

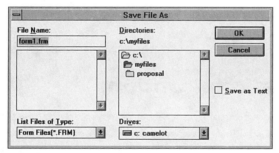

**Figure 8.4**
The Save File As dialog box.

Follow these steps to save a component file for the first time:

1. Select the component (for example, a form) to be saved to make it active.

2. Choose Save File from the Visual Basic File menu.

   The Save File As dialog box appears, as in Figure 8.4.

3. Type a name for the file.

   Navigate in the drive and directory lists to select a location for it.

4. Click OK to save the file.

After you first save a module, you can choose Save File at any point to save changes you may have made to the module. Changes are saved immediately without the intervention of a dialog box.

### Save File As

You can use the Save File As command to create a copy of an existing element. This copy is immediately substituted for the original file, keeping you from having to remove it and replace it with a copy.

To work with a copy of a module in a project, rather than the original, follow these steps:

1. Click the module's name on the Project window to select the original to copy.

2. Choose Save File As from the File menu.

3. Type a new name and location in the dialog box that appears, and then click OK.

# Setting Operational Options

You have more control over a Visual Basic project than just naming and locating it. Visual Basic has options that control how individual projects are handled, and how the program as a whole behaves. We'll look at the latter topic first.

### Environment Options

You can set a wide variety of Visual Basic environmental operation options using the Environment Options dialog box. You get to this dialog box by choosing Environment from the Visual Basic Options menu. The results of doing so are shown in Figure 8.5.

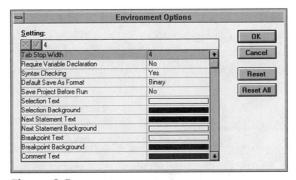

**Figure 8.5**
The Environment Options dialog box.

Environment options include:

☐ Whether to show a grid in design mode; you can use this grid to line up controls

☐ Settings for the width and height of the grid, if any

☐ Whether to align controls to the grid

☐ Whether to check for syntax errors while code is being entered

☐ Whether to require variables be declared in all modules in a program

☐ Whether to save all files before running

Take the following steps to change Environment options:

1. Choose Environment from the Visual Basic Options menu.

   The Environment Options dialog box appears.

2. Click to select the option settings you want.

3. Click OK to put changes into effect.

Any changes you make will apply to any and all projects unless you change the Environment options again.

## Code Format Options

An important subset of Environment options affects how the Code window appears; in particular, it affects how Visual Basic displays different kinds of text. You set these options using the Environment Options dialog box, as shown in Figure 8.6.

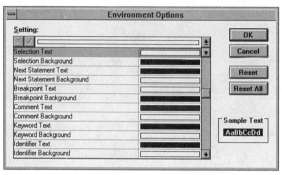

### Figure 8.6

Environment Options for the Code window; note the Sample Text item that shows the results of your choices.

Code format Environment options include:

☐ The Foreground and Background colors used to show Visual Basic keywords and your comments

☐ Text colors used to show selections

☐ Text colors used to highlight erroneous code lines in Break mode

☐ The tab width to set for the autoindent feature, if used

Take the following steps to change Code format options:

1. Choose Environment from the Visual Basic Options menu.

   The Environment Options dialog box appears.

2. Click to select an option setting you want to change.

3. Click the down-arrow icon to the left of the edit box, at the top of the dialog box.

   This drops down a list of choices. Click to select the one you want.

4. Click OK to put changes into effect.

Any changes you make will apply to any and all projects unless you change the Format options again.

## Project Options

Finally, there are options you can set that affect only the current project. These options are saved along with the project, and appear whenever that project is open. These options appear in the Project Options dialog box, accessed by way of the Project command in the Options menu. Figure 8.7 shows this dialog box.

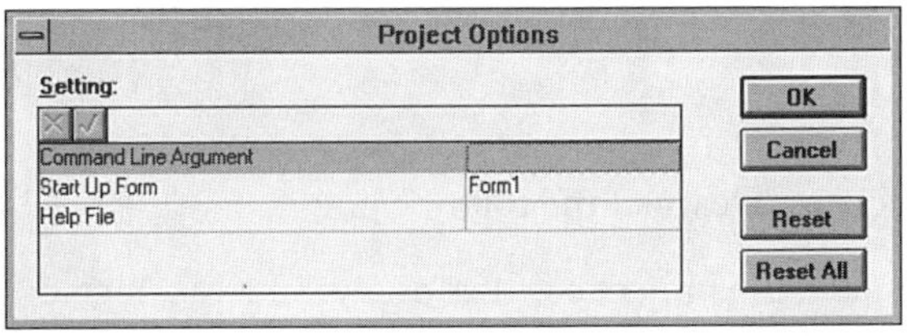

**Figure 8.7**
The Project Options dialog box.

Project options include:

☐ The form to use when the project starts up at run time

☐ Command-line arguments for the project. These are for testing purposes at design time. This subject is beyond the scope of this book; you needn't include command-line arguments anyway

☐ The name of any Help file associated with the project

Take the following steps to change Project options:

1. Choose Project Options from the Visual Basic Tools menu.

   The Project Options dialog box appears.

2. Click to select the option settings you want to change.

3. Click the drop-down list at the top of the dialog box to see options.

4. Choose or type an option; click the checkmark icon, if it's not dimmed, to put changes into effect. If the checkmark is dimmed, the change already has been made.

5. Click OK to close the dialog box.

Any changes you make will apply to this project unless you change the Project options again. Settings for other projects are not affected.

**Note** You can return all settings to their normal (default) values using the Reset All button on either the Environment Options dialog box, shown in Figure 8.5, or the Project Options dialog box, shown in Figure 8.7. You can use the Reset button to switch the currently selected option back to its original setting. The default values for all selections are those chosen by Microsoft. If you make a change in a setting, make a subsequent change to it, and then choose Reset, you get the original Microsoft setting and not your first change.

# Review

In this lesson, you learned the following:

☐ A Visual Basic project consists of several parts, including form (.FRM) files, standard module (.BAS) files, and a single .MAK or project file that references the others.

☐ You save a project and its constituent parts using the Save Project and Save File commands, respectively.

☐ An existing project is opened for editing using the Open Project command in the File menu.

☐ You can create copies of a project and of its constituent parts using the Save Project As and Save File As commands, respectively.

☐ The Environment Options dialog box is used to set global options for how Visual Basic looks and behaves. The Project Options dialog box sets options for the current project only.

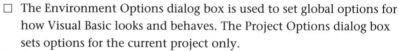

**Quiz**

Now you should be ready for the quiz.

# Part II
## Intermediate Topics

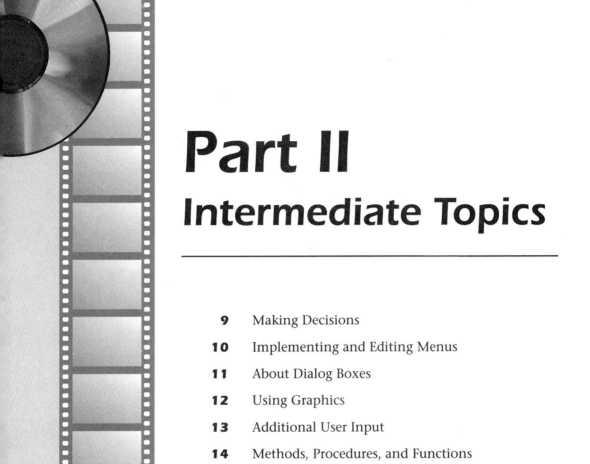

# Lesson 9

# Making Decisions

## Overview

A computer program is a kind of recipe to accomplish something, so you might think of it as being executed one step after another. Frequently this is true, but sometimes it's necessary to deviate from the established order. Suppose, for example, that in the middle of following a recipe, you discover you're out of butter. Is it acceptable to substitute something else? If so, are there any other changes you'll need to make in the way the recipe is followed after making that substitution? If we test a condition (is there butter?) and based upon the result (no), we make a decision (substitute shortening, reduce the amount of liquid), then we are practicing the same kind of decision-making process that makes a sophisticated computer program more useful than a program that merely performs one task after another, step-by-step, plunging ahead without ever "thinking" about what should happen next.

The ability to deal with different possibilities gives a computer program much of its power. Typically, you'll find it necessary to perform some sort of test on an item of data, and then make a decision on how to handle it based on the test results. Consider a program that finds the simple interest on an outstanding balance. Multiplying the balance by the interest rate would give you the answer, *unless* the balance is negative; in this case the interest is simply zero. So in this example, we first must test the balance to see if it is greater than zero. If it is, the formula determines the interest. If it isn't, the interest is simply zero.

The kinds of decisions described in the preceding paragraph can be carried out in Visual Basic statements like those introduced in Lesson 7, "Manipulating Data: Expressions and Operations." The decision-making statements in Visual Basic are called *control structures* because they control how a program is executed. There are several types of control structures; we'll discuss each in this lesson.

This lesson covers the following points about making decisions in Visual Basic:

☐ Reasons for changing the typical way programs are carried out

☐ Statements for performing either one set of actions or another set of actions

☐ Statements for repeating a certain set of actions a specific number of times, or an indefinite number of times

# Controlling the Flow of a Program

Although it sounds slightly militaristic, we refer to programs as being *executed*. This is just another way of saying that your computer runs programs. Typically, a program executes in a specified way. However, it is possible to build statements into a program to change the typical execution sequence. There are some important reasons for doing so. We describe program execution and reasons for changing it in the following two sections.

### How Programs Are Executed

As a rule, your computer executes a program one step at a time, taking each statement within a procedure in sequence. In an event-driven environment such as Visual Basic, pretty much nothing happens between procedures; typically the program is waiting for the user to do something else. Figure 9.1 shows a Visual Basic program with a typical sequence of event procedures assigned to two different command buttons.

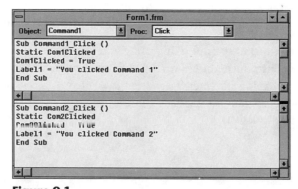

**Figure 9.1**
Two Visual Basic procedures with statements; they will execute in order.

**Note** If you'd like to be able to see two procedures at once, as shown in Figure 9.1, you can "split" the code window. Move the mouse pointer over the bottom part of the code window's header; the mouse pointer turns into a double-headed vertical arrow. Click and drag down to about halfway down the code window; this splits the window. You can set each part of the window to show a different procedure; click in a code window part and use the Object and Proc drop-down menus. Note the single line that appears at the top of the lower window; drag this line all the way up to merge the two displays back into one.

Here's what happens in the Figure 9.1 example when the user clicks `Command1`.

1. A static variable named `Com1Clicked` is created. Because it is static, this variable remains in existence outside the `Command1` procedure. The variable is variant in type, meaning it can contain (in this application) the value True or False.

2. The variable `Com1Clicked` is given the value True.

3. The label `Label1` is set to read `You clicked Command 1`.

In between command button clicks, this program does nothing; no statements are executed. Can you figure out what happens if the user clicks `Command2`? In this case, the variable `Com2Clicked` is given the value True, and `Label1` is set to read `You clicked Command 2`.

In both cases, the static variable created and then given the value True doesn't seem to be of much use. This, however, is about to change.

## Reasons for Changing Program Flow

When is the typical top-to-bottom, one-statement-after-the-other organization not adequate? One case is where we might want to execute one statement in one case, and another statement in some other case. Suppose, for example, we wanted to put a different statement into the example from Figure 9.1 if the user had clicked a key once already? Because we have a variable, `Com1Clicked`, which is set to True after this has happened, we need only to test it, and then specify what to do if the test is met. Figure 9.2 shows the same procedures with such a test added.

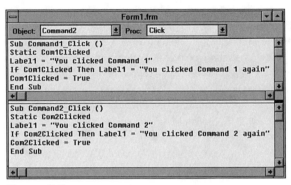

**Figure 9.2**
Modifying the two Visual Basic procedures to test if the buttons have been clicked before.

Here's what happens in the Figure 9.2 example when the user clicks Command1 *twice*.

1. A static variable named Com1Clicked is created. This variable remains in existence outside the Command1 procedure.

   The variable is Variant in type, meaning it can contain the value True or False.

2. The label Label1 is set to read You clicked Command 1.

3. The value of Com1Clicked is tested to see if it is True. It has never been given a value the first time the button is clicked, so it isn't True. The rest of the statement is skipped.

4. The variable Com1Clicked is given the value True.

5. On the second click, the procedure is executed again. The variable doesn't have to be re-created, because it's static.

6. The label Label1 is set to read You clicked Command 1.

7. The variable Com1Clicked is evaluated. It is true, so the rest of the statement is executed. The label is changed to read You clicked Command 1 again.

8. The variable Com1Clicked is given the value True again. Notice that this will take place even though it's redundant every time after the first time.

Can you tell what would happen if the user clicked Command1 first, then Command2, followed by Command1 again? In this case, the label finally reads You clicked Command 1 again, just as in the previous example.

In addition to executing a statement (or statements) based on a condition, (sometimes called conditional execution), it often is useful to be able to repeat a statement or group of statements. Figure 9.3, for example, shows two ways to put ordered numbers into an array.

```
┌────────────────────────────────────────────────┐
│ ─                    Form1.frm              ▼  ▲ │
│ ┌──────────────────────────────────────────────┤
│ │ Object: │Command4    │▲│ Proc: │Click      │▲│ │
│ ├──────────────────────────────────────────────┤
│ │Sub Command3_Click ()                        ▲│ │
│ │Dim CountByFive(4) As Integer                 │ │
│ │CountByFive(0) = 5                            │ │
│ │CountByFive(1) = 10                           │ │
│ │CountByFive(2) = 15                           │ │
│ │CountByFive(3) = 20                           │ │
│ │CountByFive(4) = 25                           │ │
│ │End Sub                                      ▼│ │
│ │◄│                                         │►│  │
│ ├──────────────────────────────────────────────┤
│ │Sub Command4_Click ()                        ▲│ │
│ │Dim CountByFive(4) As Integer                 │ │
│ │For x = 0 To 4                                │ │
│ │CountByFive(x) = (x * 5) + 5                  │ │
│ │Next x                                        │ │
│ │End Sub                                      ▼│ │
│ │◄│                                         │►│  │
│ └──────────────────────────────────────────────┘
```

**Figure 9.3**
Filling an array with multiple statements, then doing the same with a loop.

Here's what happens in the Figure 9.3 example when the user clicks Command3.

1. An array named CountByFive is created. This array has five elements, and is of type Integer.

2. The first element of CountByFive is given the value 5.

3. In the next four statements, succeeding elements of CountByFive are given values of increasing multiples of five.

Contrast this with what happens when the user clicks Command4. Take our word for it; the results are exactly the same: a five-member array containing multiples of five from 5 to 25. (The central block of three statements, from For through Next, is executed once for each possible value of x from 0 to 4; hence it executes five times.) Yet the second example uses only three statements to accomplish what took five in the first. Imagine if the array had 100 elements. It still would only take three statements to fill it, using procedures similar to those shown for Command4. Clearly this is easier than assigning values one at a time.

# Statements to Control Program Execution

The preceding examples have introduced the notion of using certain statements to control the execution of a program. These types of statements fall into one of the three broad categories of Visual Basic statements, the others being variable creation statements and assignment statements. As the example shows, there are in turn two broad categories of control structure statements: conditionally executed statements, and loops.

## Simple Conditional Execution: If...Then Statements

Figure 9.2 showed an example of the easiest conditionally executed statement—the If...Then statement. Such a statement takes the form:

```
If expression Then statement
```

In this syntax, *expression* is a logical expression, which evaluates to either True or False, and *statement* is some other Visual Basic statement, usually an assignment statement like that shown in the example. The statement is executed if and only if the expression is true. If the expression is not true, the statement is skipped.

The following are examples of simple conditionally executed statements using If...Then:

```
If IsMiddleAged Then Label1 = "You're getting over the hill."
If (Age<65 AND Age>49) Then Label1 = "You're middle aged."


If (Balance<0) Then Balance=0
```

The first example only works if IsMiddleAged is a variant variable set to True. For the second example to work, Age must be a numeric variable whose value is less than 65 but greater than 49 (in other words, 50 through 64). In the last example, the value of the variable Balance is set to 0 if it was previously less than 0; otherwise, nothing happens.

### Executing Several Statements Based upon One Condition: If...Then Blocks

Often it's necessary to execute more than one statement based on the results of a single test. You could, of course, simply repeat the test the appropriate number of times, replacing the statement to be executed in each instance. A simpler method, however, is to have all the statements executed in a block. Figure 9.4 shows just such a block.

```
┌──────────────────────────────────────────────────┐
│ ─              Form1.frm                    ▼ ▲   │
│ ┌──────────────────────────────────────────────┐ │
│ │ Object: │Command1      │▼│ Proc: │Click    │▼│ │
│ ├──────────────────────────────────────────────┤ │
│ │Sub Command1_Click ()                       │▲│ │
│ │Static Com1Clicked                            │ │
│ │Label1 = "You clicked Command 1"              │ │
│ │If Com1Clicked Then                           │ │
│ │Label1 = "You clicked Command 1 again"        │ │
│ │Command1.Caption = "Not Again"                │ │
│ │End If                                        │ │
│ │Com1Clicked = True                            │ │
│ │End Sub                                       │ │
│ │                                              │ │
│ │                                            │▼│ │
│ ├──────────────────────────────────────────────┤ │
│ │◄│                                          │►│ │
│ └──────────────────────────────────────────────┘ │
└──────────────────────────────────────────────────┘
```

If block

**Figure 9.4**
Executing multiple statements based on one test.

The general form of an `If...Then` block of statements is:

```
If expression Then
     statement1
     statement2
     ...
     statementLast
End If
```

The statement `End If` at the end of the block of statements is critical; it tells Visual Basic the block is over.

### Either-Or Choices: Using If...Then...Else

It also may be the case that you want to execute another statement or group of statements if the condition evaluated in an `If...Then` statement turns out to be false. You do so by adding the keyword `Else` to the typical `If...Then` statement. The statement(s) after `Else` is/are executed only if the expression tested evaluates to "false." Figure 9.5 shows the previous example rewritten to take advantage of `Else`.

The general form of an `If...Then...Else` block of statements is:

```
If expression Then
     statement1
     statement2
     ...
     statementLast
Else
     statementelse1
     statementelse2
     ...
     statementelselast
End If
```

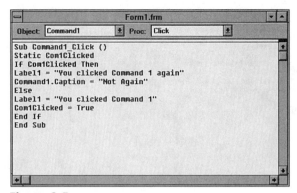

**Figure 9.5**
Executing an If block or an alternative, based on one test.

Of course, it's possible to specify only a single statement for both If and Else, as in If expression Then statement1 Else statement2. Such a statement can be placed on a single line.

### Choices Based on Multiple Conditions: Nesting If...Thens

One (or more) of the statements within an If...Then...Else block actually can be another If...Then...Else statement. This enables you to set up some really complicated conditions to evaluate. The process of including If...Then statements within each other is called *nesting*. Figure 9.6 shows an example of nested If...Thens.

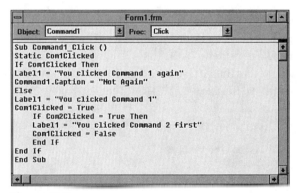

**Figure 9.6**
Nested If...Thens.

## More (and Easier) Multiple Conditions: Select Case

While you could use quite a series of nested If...Thens to set up a sort of multiple choice scenario, Visual Basic offers an easier way to select one set of options from among several to execute. The relevant statement is Select Case. In this instance, the test expression to be evaluated generally yields a numeric (in fact, integer) result. Figure 9.7 shows an example of a Select Case structure.

```
Form1.frm
Object: Command1        Proc: Click

Sub Command1_Click ()
Static X
X = X + 1
Select Case X
    Case 1
        Label1 = "You clicked Command 1 once"
    Case 2
        Label1 = "You clicked Command 1 twice"
    Case Else
        Label1 = "You clicked Command 1 more than twice"
End Select
End Sub
```

**Figure 9.7**
Using Select Case to make decisions.

The general form of a Select Case block of statements is:

```
Select Case testexpression
Case value1
    statement1
    statement2
    ...
    statementLast
Case value2
    statementvalue21
    statementvalue22
    ...
    statementvalue2last
...
Case Else
    statementelse1
    statementelse2
    ...
    statementelselast
End Select
```

Of course, it's possible to specify only a single statement for each case.

The relevant block of statements is executed, depending on the value yielded by the test expression. If none of the cases matches the test expression, then the statements under `Case Else` are executed. Note that, as with `If...Then` blocks, the `Case Else` statement is optional and can be omitted. If it is omitted, and none of the cases matches the test expression, then nothing happens.

# Executing Statements Multiple Times: Looping

At times you may not want to execute alternative blocks of statements; instead, you may want to execute the same block of statements multiple times. Earlier in this lesson we discussed reasons why this can be useful. Visual Basic offers two ways to loop: `For...Next` loops, and `Do` loops, of which in turn there are two types, `Do...While` and `Do...Until`.

### For...Next Loops

Your basic `For...Next` loop performs a set of actions a given number of times. The number of times specified doesn't have to be a constant value; it can be a variable's contents, or even an expression.

The general form of a `For...Next` loop is:

```
For indexvariable = startvalueexpression To endvalueexpression
          [Step stepvalueexpression]
    statement1
    statement2
    ...
    statementlast
Next indexvariable
```

Figure 9.3 showed an example of using a `For...Next` loop to fill an array. In that case, the relevant statements were:

```
For x = 0 to 4
CountByFive(x) = (x*5)+5
Next x
```

Note that in this case, the `Step` keyword is omitted. If you omit `Step`, then Visual Basic assumes you want to count by 1. You can count backward if you want (sometimes it's even necessary). To do so, specify a `Step` of -1. The following example does the same thing as the previous one:

```
For x = 4 to 0 Step -1
CountByFive(x) = (x*5)+5
Next x
```

In general, a For...Next loop executes as follows:

1. The index variable is set equal to its initial value.

2. The block of statements above the Next statement is executed once.

3. The Step amount is added to the amount in the index variable.

4. The index variable is tested to see if it exceeds the end value. If not, the loop is repeated.

5. Step 4 is repeated until the index variable's contents exceed the end value; then the loop stops. The next statement (if any) after the loop (after the Next statement) is executed.

## Do Loops

Visual Basic has other looping statements that depend on logical conditions rather than the numeric values used by For...Next loops. Such structures are called Do loops. There are two kinds of Do loops. One executes as long as a given expression is true; another executes until a given expression is true. Figure 9.8 shows an example of each.

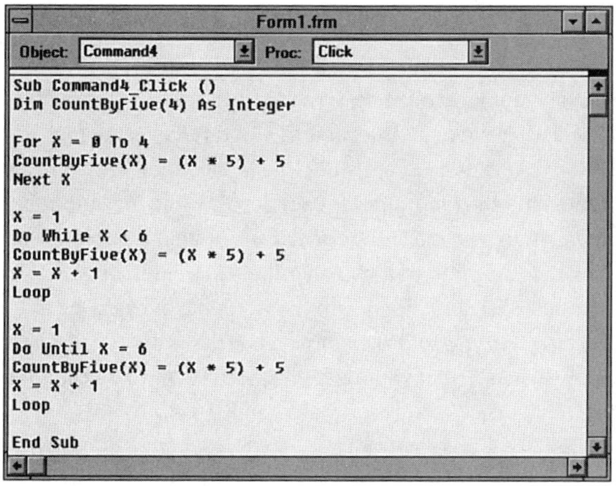

```
 ─                          Form1.frm                      ▼ ▲
 Object:  Command4        ±  Proc:  Click              ±
 Sub Command4_Click ()                                    ↑
 Dim CountByFive(4) As Integer

 For X = 0 To 4
 CountByFive(X) = (X * 5) + 5
 Next X

 X = 1
 Do While X < 6
 CountByFive(X) = (X * 5) + 5
 X = X + 1
 Loop

 X = 1
 Do Until X = 6
 CountByFive(X) = (X * 5) + 5
 X = X + 1
 Loop

 End Sub                                                  ↓
 ←                                                       →
```

**Figure 9.8**
For...Next, Do While, and Do Until loops that do the same thing.

### Do While

A Do While loop executes as long as a test condition evaluates to True. In the example shown in Figure 9.8, the loop executes while the value of the variable x is less than 6.

The general form of a Do While loop is the following:

```
Do While testexpression
      statement1
      statement2
      ...
      statement3
Loop
```

In general, a Do While loop executes as follows:

1. The test expression is evaluated. If it is true, the block of statements beneath it is executed. If not, control passes to the next statement after the loop, and the following steps 2 and 3 do not apply.

2. After all statements are executed once, the test expression is evaluated again.

3. If the test expression is still true, the block of statements is repeated, and after all statements are executed, the test expression is evaluated again.

   This step is repeated until the test expression finally is evaluated as false, at which point control passes to the next statement after the loop.

**Caution** Something within your loop must do something to alter the value of the test expression. Otherwise, it will always remain true, and the loop will execute forever. We call such a structure an *infinite loop*. A program stuck in a infinite loop just seems to hang there. The procedure containing the loop is never completed, while the loop repeats endlessly, chewing up resources. Your humble author once came within a single comma of submitting a program to a large computer that had an infinite loop in it, one that would have bankrupted his computer account along with the accounts of everyone else in his 200-member programming class. He was told later this occurrence would have merited an immediate "F" in the class. Should one of your own programs seem to be caught in such a loop, press Ctrl+Break.

### Do Until

Do Until is exactly the same as saying Do While Not. Such a loop executes until the test condition is true; in effect, it executes as long as the test condition is false. The loop doesn't execute at all if the test expression is immediately found to be true.

The general form of a `Do Until` loop is the following:

```
Do Until testexpression
     statement1
     statement2
     ...
     statement3
Loop
```

## Getting Out of a Loop

At times you may want to leave a loop prematurely. For example, if you're searching an array for a particular value, you don't need to continue searching through the rest of the array once you've found it. Using the `Exit` statement, you can get out of any loop whenever you need to. Figure 9.9 shows a loop containing an `Exit` statement that forces the program to leave the loop once the location of a specific value is found.

```
Form1.frm
Object: Command4      Proc: Click

Sub Command4_Click ()
Dim CountByFive(4) As Integer

For X = 0 To 4
CountByFive(X) = (X * 5) + 5
Next X

For X = 0 To 4
  If CountByFive(X) = 20 Then
     Label1 = X
     Exit For
  End If
Next X
```

**Figure 9.9**
Exiting a `For...Next` loop before it's done.

You must include the type of structure you're exiting as part of the `Exit` statement. To exit a `For...Next` loop, use `Exit For`. To exit either of the `Do` loops, use `Exit Do`.

## Nesting Loops

As with `If...Then` statements, you can nest loops within each other. This is handy, for example, when working with multidimensional arrays, as the example in Figure 9.10 shows.

II

Intermediate Topics

```
┌──────────────────────────────────────────────────┐
│ ⊟                    Form1.frm                 ▼ ▲ │
├──────────────────────────────────────────────────┤
│ Object: │Command4       │▲│ Proc: │Click      │▲│ │
├──────────────────────────────────────────────────┤
│ Sub Command4_Click ()                          ▲  │
│ Dim CountByFive(4, 1) As Integer                  │
│                                                   │
│ For X = 0 To 4                                    │
│     For Y = 0 To 1                                │
│     CountByFive(X, Y) = ((X + Y) * 5) + 5         │
│     Next Y                                        │
│ Next X                                            │
│                                                   │
│ End Sub                                           │
│                                                ▼  │
├──────────────────────────────────────────────────┤
│ ◄│                                             │►│ │
└──────────────────────────────────────────────────┘
```

**Figure 9.10**
Nested For...Next loops.

Remember the following when you use nested loops:

☐ You can nest as many levels deep as you want or need to.

☐ Indenting each successive level one tab stop further than the last level makes your code easier to read.

☐ Be sure to close each successive loop *before* closing the one within which it's nested. Closing an outer loop before you close a loop within it is called *crossing* loops, and Visual Basic won't let you do so.

# Review

In this lesson, you learned the following:

☐ Statements that alter the flow of program execution are called control structures.

☐ Use If...Then...Else statements to conditionally execute blocks of statements based on the truth or falsity of a test expression.

☐ Use the Select Case structure to execute one of several blocks of statements, based on the numerical value of a test expression.

☐ Use `For...Next` loops to execute a block of statements a given number of times.

☐ The `Do While` and `Do Until` loop structures are used to execute blocks of statements while a test condition is true, or until it becomes true, respectively.

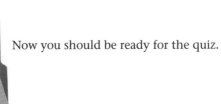

Now you should be ready for the quiz.

## Lesson 10

# Implementing and Editing Menus

## Overview

Is there any part of a modern user interface more important than menus? For many people, the presence of well-organized menus is the most important part of a graphical user interface. Indeed, menus have become so much of a user expectation that a Microsoft Windows application can hardly succeed without them. Fortunately, programming menus is no longer difficult. Visual Basic has centralized and automated much of what it takes to make a menu. In this lesson, we show you how to use this capability to add menus of commands to your own Visual Basic projects.

This lesson covers the following points regarding menus:

☐ The organized groups of commands with which menus are associated

☐ How to create a menu for a form

☐ How to use the Menu Design Editor to alter an existing form menu

☐ How to associate procedures with each command in a menu

## About Menus

A menu is a list of associated commands. Within all good Microsoft Windows programs, menus appear along the menu bar at the top of the program's window. Figure 10.1 shows the menu bar for Visual Basic itself.

Menu bar—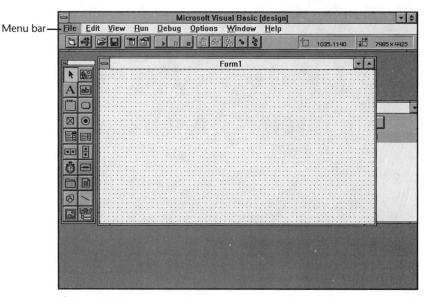

**Figure 10.1**
Visual Basic's menu bar contains several drop-down menus.

## Uses and Types of Menus

Typically, menus are used to organize most of the commands within an application program. While less important commands may be accessed in some other way, the most commonly used commands are always in menus.

If you look at several typical Microsoft Windows applications, you'll see several menus that appear time and time again. These menus are summarized in the following table:

| Menu | Commands |
| --- | --- |
| File | Open, save, print, and close files, and quit the application |
| Edit | Cut and copy items to the Clipboard, and paste them from it. May contain commands to search for and or replace items |
| Format | Change the appearance of items on-screen, usually data items such as text |
| Tools | Accomplish special, sometimes rather involved tasks |
| Window | In applications that let you have more than one document window open, commands in this menu let you move between windows |
| Help | Access online help, and get information about the program |

Specific applications might feature other menus in addition to these, and might be missing some others (such as Tools and Window). All well-behaved Windows applications should have File and Edit menus, and probably a Help menu as well.

## Typical Menu Organization

Within a menu, commands usually are presented in a logical and well organized manner. Figure 10.2 shows the File menu within Visual Basic.

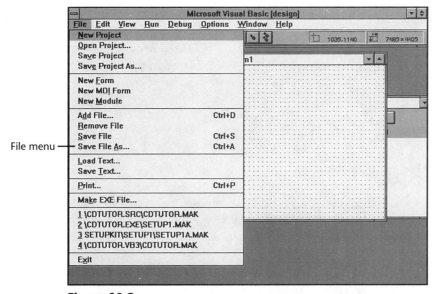

**Figure 10.2**
Visual Basic's File menu, dropped down.

Take a close look at the Visual Basic File menu, keeping in mind these points:

☐ Like commands are kept together; notice how all the Save commands (Save File, Save Project, and so forth) appear in one group.

☐ Groups of four (usually) or fewer like commands are separated from one another with bars.

☐ Commands that always bring up dialog boxes are followed by ellipses, as in Save File As....

☐ The order in which groups of commands appear reflects in some way the organization of the program. In the case of the File menu, first you create a new project, then you save it, then you add or remove items, then you print results, then you quit.

☐ Each menu command has a hotkey, which lets the user access the command from the keyboard without touching the mouse. In each menu command, the hotkey is underlined. The user presses the Alt key, followed by the hotkey for the menu, followed by the hotkey for the command.

☐ The most important menu commands have keyboard shortcuts. These may either be a combination of Ctrl and another key or can be one of the function keys like F4 or F7. The user presses the appropriate keyboard shortcut to execute the associated command.

☐ The Exit command, to leave the program, is always last.

# Creating a Menu

Although creating your own menus may seem complex, Visual Basic actually makes it quite simple. The program features a powerful menu editor. Using it, you can create a separate set of menus for each form in a project.

### Using the Visual Basic Menu Design Window

You access the Visual Basic Menu Design window through the Menu Design command in the Visual Basic Window menu. When you do so for the first time in a project, you'll see a dialog box something like Figure 10.3.

Within this window, you see places to enter both the Caption and the Name for a menu command; the Caption is what the user sees, and the Name is how you refer to the menu command within your Visual Basic code. There are buttons to insert and delete new menu names and menu commands, as well as buttons to change their position. Overall menu organization appears within a panel at the bottom of the dialog box.

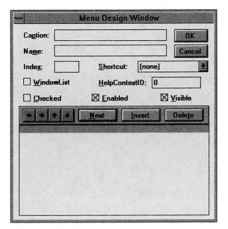

**Figure 10.3**
Visual Basic's Menu Design window; there is no menu yet for this form.

Take the following steps to access the Menu Design window:

1. With the appropriate project open, use the Project window to display the form for which you want to add or change menus.

2. Choose Menu Design from the Visual Basic Window menu, or press Ctrl+M.

3. The Menu Design window appears. Note that although called a window, it performs like a dialog box—you can't click off it to make another part of Visual Basic active. You must close the Menu Design window first, either by clicking OK, or by clicking Cancel or the Close box.

### Adding Menu Names and Menu Commands

Figure 10.4 shows what the Menu Design window looks like with a very simple set of menus and commands. There are only two menus, File and Edit. Each menu contains only a few commands.

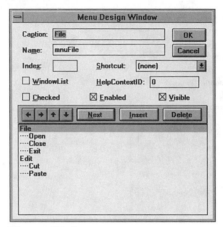

**Figure 10.4**
Visual Basic's Menu Design window showing two simple menus.

Notice that menu names appear flush left in the scrolling area at the bottom of the screen. Commands appear indented underneath the menu to which they belong. You use the right-facing arrow key to indent an item, making it a command rather than a menu. The captions for each menu name and menu command are exactly as they appear on the form's menu bar. The command names, however, are somewhat more complicated. Although you can give menus and menu commands any valid Visual Basic name you want, you might want to use a little organization. We've preceded each item name with the three letters "mnu" to show it's in a menu. Although you can't see it in Figure 10.4, menu commands also include the name of the menu in which they appear, as well as their captions. Thus, the Cut and Paste commands in the Edit menu have the names

```
mnuEdit_Cut
mnuEdit_Paste
```

Note the underscore used to separate parts of each name. You don't have to do this, but it makes your code easier to read and understand. You cannot, however, separate the parts of a menu command name with blank spaces.

Take the following steps to add an item to a menu:

1. With the appropriate project open, use the Project window to display the form for which you want to add or change menu items.

2. Choose Menu Design from the Visual Basic Window menu, or press Ctrl+M.

   The Menu Design window appears.

3. In the scrolling area at the bottom of the screen, click to select the item before which you want to insert the new item.

   This and the following step isn't necessary if you're creating a new menu.

4. Click the Insert button.

5. Type a caption for the item in the Caption text edit box.

6. Type a name for the item in the Name text edit box.

   Recall that the name is what Visual Basic will use to reference the menu or menu command within your program code.

7. If you're adding a menu command, click the right-facing arrow to indent the command. It will be preceded by four dots after you do so.

8. Click the OK key to put changes into effect.

### Enabling Keystrokes

Although computer mice have been the wave of the future for quite some time past (the implicit irony in this statement is intended), there are still those who prefer to use the keyboard to enter commands whenever possible. There's good reason for this: most folks work with their fingers on the keys. Reaching over for the mouse takes time and effort; it's faster and easier just to type.

Recognizing this, Microsoft gives the user the ability to access menus and menu commands directly from the keyboard in all their Windows application programs. Microsoft does this by adding hotkeys and or command-key equivalents for menu commands. Any well-behaved Windows program—such as your own Visual Basic project—is expected to do the same.

**Adding Hotkeys to a Menu** According to Microsoft, each menu and menu command has a *hotkey*; this is a single keystroke that, when pressed after the user presses the Alt key, accesses the menu or menu command just as if the user had clicked it with the mouse. (Note that for menu commands, the user must first press Alt, then the hotkey for the menu containing the command.) Hotkeys are underlined. Figure 10.5 shows hotkeys added to the menu we've been working with. Pay particular attention to the ampersand character (&), which precedes the hotkey for a command.

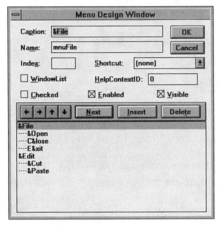

**Figure 10.5**
Adding hotkeys to menus and menu items.

Follow these steps to enable a hotkey for a specific menu item:

1. With the appropriate project open, use the Project window to display the form for which you want to add or change menu items.

2. Choose Menu Design from the Visual Basic Window menu, or press Ctrl+M.

   The Menu Design window appears.

3. In the scrolling area at the bottom of the screen, click to select the item to which you want to add a hotkey.

4. Click in the Caption text edit box to move the insertion point to the left of the letter you want to be the hotkey.

5. Type an ampersand character (&).

6. Repeat steps 3 through 5 for each item to which you want to add a hotkey.

7. Click OK to put changes into effect.

You can, if you want, enable hotkeys at the time you create a new menu or menu command. Just type an ampersand as part of the item's caption.

**Note**   Keep in mind that within each menu, each command must have a unique hotkey; you can't use the same letter for two different commands! This applies to menu names along the menu bar as well. Although your program won't crash if you use redundant hotkeys, only the first command is executed when the user presses the redundant hotkey; the second and any others are ignored.

**Adding Command-Key Equivalents**   For certain commands that are used quite often, some folks don't even want to mess with the Alt key or with dropping down menus at all. To honor this preference, most Microsoft Windows applications give the user command-key equivalents for several menu commands. (There are never command-key equivalents to drop-down menus.) Issuing a command-key equivalent for a menu item involves holding down the Ctrl key and typing a single letter (possibly with the Shift key held down as well). A common example is Ctrl+X to cut an item to the Clipboard. Figure 10.6 shows two command keys added to our running example.

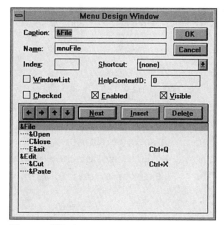

**Figure 10.6**
Adding command-key equivalents to menu items.

Follow these steps to enable a command-key equivalent for a specific menu item:

1. With the appropriate project open, use the Project window to display the form for which you want to add or change menu items.

2. Choose Menu Design from the Visual Basic Window menu, or press Ctrl+M.

   The Menu Design window appears.

3. In the scrolling area at the bottom of the screen, click to select the item to which you want to add a command key.

4. Click the Shortcut drop-down list.

   A list of possible command-key equivalents appears.

5. Scroll in the list until the appropriate command-key equivalent appears. Click to select the command-key equivalent you want.

6. Click OK to put changes into effect.

Command keys appear to the right of any menu command for which they've been enabled; this lets the user know they're available.

**Note**   Keep in mind that each potential command-key equivalent can be assigned to only one command in the entire menu bar; you can't have Ctrl+X mean both "Cut" and "Exit." If you try to assign the same command-key equivalent to two or more commands, Visual Basic displays an alert box when you click the Menu Design window's OK button. You'll have to change the redundant assignment.

## Enabling Menu Commands

After all this work you'll have a decent looking menu bar that does next to nothing. Menus will drop down when you click them, but nothing will happen if you select menu commands. You must enable them as you would any command object in Visual Basic: by writing code for them. Figure 10.7 shows code written for the File_Exit command in our running example.

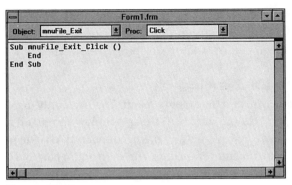

**Figure 10.7**
Enabling the Exit command in the File menu for Form1.

Follow these steps to enable a specific menu command:

1. With the appropriate project open, use the Project window to display the form for which you want to enable menu items.

2. Click the form's menu bar to display the menu containing the command to enable.

3. Click to select the command.

   The Code window appears, with a procedure header and footer for the appropriate menu command name.

4. Type Visual Basic programming code to accomplish the task for which the menu command is intended.

5. Double-click the Code window's control menu icon to close it when you're done.

# Making Changes to a Menu

If you've worked in Windows for very long, you should have noticed that certain menus change as you work within a program. Items sometimes have checkmarks next to them, to show they've been selected. (This is generally true of a command that may be "on" or "off," such as a particular kind of formatting.) Items that aren't available may appear in dim gray. And sometimes, commands disappear altogether. Not all changes to menus need happen while a program runs, however. You also can edit an existing menu before a program runs, adding, deleting, or modifying existing commands.

### Editing an Existing Menu

It's quite easy to edit an existing menu. You need only display the appropriate form, and choose the Menu Design window command again. You can add and delete new menus and menu commands, change the order of existing menus and menu commands, and even add separator bars between groups of commands.

Follow these steps to edit an existing menu:

1. With the appropriate project open, use the Project window to display the form for which you want to edit menu items.

2. Choose the Menu Design command from the Window menu, or press Ctrl+M.

3. Click to select the item to edit, or before which you want to add an item.

4. Use the arrow keys to change the selected item's position. Click Delete to remove the item; click Insert to put a new item before it.

5. Click OK to put the changes into effect.

**Note** To add a separator bar between commands, click to select the command that the bar should appear above. Click Insert, give the new item a single hyphen as a caption and a unique name such as Bar1, and then click OK. Figure 10.8 shows the effects of just such an operation.

### Changes on the Fly: Giving the User Feedback

As with all other command objects, Visual Basic menus and menu commands have properties. You can use several of these properties to make changes to a menu as a program runs. This gives the user some visual feedback as the program progresses. Figure 10.9 shows a menu that has had two such changes made to it during run time.

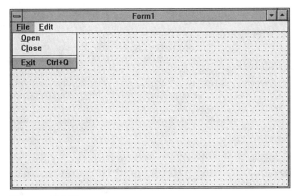

**Figure 10.8**
A separator bar between the Close and Exit commands in the File menu.

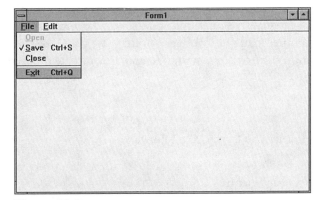

**Figure 10.9**
Checked and dimmed items in the File menu.

Use the following menu command properties to change how (or if) the command appears as a program runs:

| Property | Effects |
|---|---|
| Checked | If this property is set to True, a checkmark appears next to the command's name. The checkmark persists until this property is set to False. |
| Enabled | If this property is set to True, the command can be accessed. If this property is set to False, the command will be dimmed out; nothing will happen if the user attempts to select it. The command remains dimmed until Enabled is reset to True. |

(continues)

| Property | Effects |
| --- | --- |
| Visible | If this property is set to True, the command appears in the menu. If this property is set to False, the command will not appear in the menu, and nothing will happen if the user attempts to access it by way of hotkey or command-key equivalents. The command remains inaccessible until the property is reset to True. |

As with any property, you use periods to separate the property name from the command name when referencing it. Thus, the commands to check the Save menu and dim the Open menu from the example in Figure 10.9 are:

```
mnuFile_Save.Checked = True
mnuFile_Open.Enabled = False
```

You can include these commands in any procedure in which it makes sense to do so. Frequently something you do in one command, for example, may make another temporarily useless; in that case you'd use the Enabled property within the first command to temporarily disable the second.

# Review

In this lesson, you learned the following:

☐ Microsoft Windows program applications offer most of their commands in menus.

☐ Menus are named groups of commands that appear across the menu bar at the top of a program's window. Menus drop down, when selected, to reveal the names of the commands within them.

☐ You can add a single menu to any form in a project (and edit the menu once it's there) using the Menu Design window. You access this window by choosing Menu Design from the Visual Basic Window menu.

☐ Within the Menu Design window, menu commands appear indented beneath the name of the menu to which they belong.

☐ Preceding a letter in a menu command caption with an ampersand (&) makes that letter a hotkey for the command. Hotkeys are activated after the user presses Alt. You may also associate a command-key combination with any command. These are chosen from the Shortcuts drop-down list.

☐ Menu commands are enabled, like any other command object, by having procedures written for them.

☐ Menu commands have properties like any other command object. The Checked, Enabled, and Visible properties are used to add a checkmark to, to dim out, and to hide menu commands, respectively.

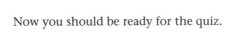

Now you should be ready for the quiz.

**II**

**Intermediate Topics**

# About Dialog Boxes

## Overview

The experienced Windows user, like yourself presumably, often has been confronted with the need to acknowledge a specific event, or to make choices within a narrowly defined context. For example, you've probably had to click the OK button to close a brief message that informed you of some error or other. You've probably also had to navigate in Drive, Directory, and File lists to choose a specific file to open, after choosing an Open File command or something like it. In both cases, you've been dealing with dialog boxes. Whenever they'll be of benefit, you can add them to your own Visual Basic programs.

This lesson covers the following points regarding dialog and alert boxes:

☐ The types of dialog boxes, and what they're used for

☐ How to enable different types of alert and input boxes

☐ About the Common Dialog control, used for opening files

## Dialog Box Types and Purposes

Dialog boxes fall into two broad categories. There are those that appear to inform the user of some fact or other. These usually have a single button, labeled OK; clicking that button closes the dialog box. This type of dialog box is sometimes called an alert box. The second type of dialog box lets the user make a choice. Frequently this dialog box has a text edit box into which the user can type a choice. This type of dialog box is sometimes called an input box. A special type of dialog box, called the Common Dialog box, lets the user navigate in the directory list (among other things) to find a specific file to act on.

## Alert Boxes

An alert box simply informs the user that something has happened. It also can be used to provide information about a program. The About This Program... command found in many applications' Help menus is an example of the latter. Figure 11.1 shows an alert box of this type, created within Visual Basic. Note the "i" icon, which is supposed to tell the user that this dialog box provides information.

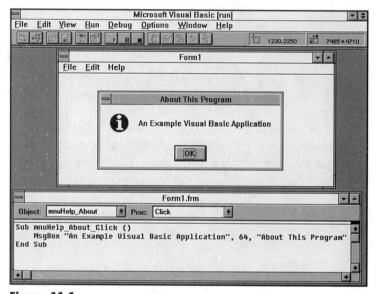

**Figure 11.1**
An alert box, with the code that created it.

The user clicks the OK button to close this dialog box, which first appears when the user chooses the About This Program... command in the Form1 Help menu. It does nothing else.

## Input Boxes

An input box is slightly more involved than an alert box. Such a dialog box lets the user type in something. As part of the code used to create the dialog box, the value typed in by the user is stored in a variable. Figure 11.2 shows an Input box.

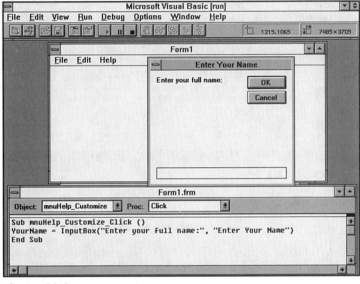

**Figure 11.2**
An input box, with the code that created it.

## Common Dialog Boxes

The most involved form of dialog boxes is the common dialog box. You're familiar with these; one appears if you choose Open or Save, if you select a font, or if you want to pick a specific color from a palette. Figures 11.3 and 11.4 show two such dialog boxes and the Visual Basic code that created them.

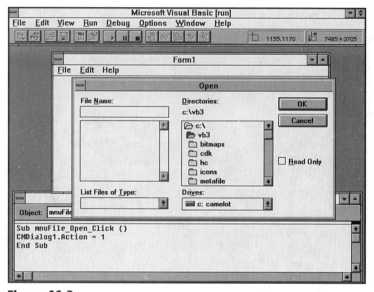

**Figure 11.3**
An Open dialog box, with the code that created it.

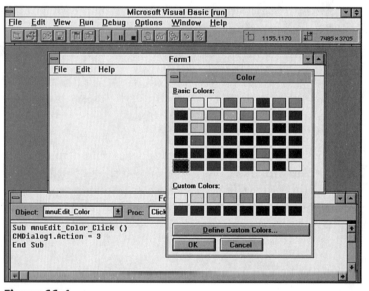

**Figure 11.4**
A Color palette dialog box, with the code that created it.

With any of the common dialog boxes, you must include the Common
Dialog command object on the appropriate form. You need only one

instance of this object. Although its icon appears on the form (you can put it anywhere), the dialog box remains invisible until activated. You need only one common dialog control per form, no matter how many different such dialog boxes you want to make available. Note that you cannot control where the dialog box appears when it is activated, although the user can drag it to a new position.

# Creating Dialog Boxes

The preceding figures showed that there are two ways to call a dialog box within your Visual Basic code, depending on which type of dialog box you want to invoke. You either can use a special, named procedure, in the case of alert and input boxes, or you can use the common dialog control, found on the toolbox.

## The MsgBox Function

Use the MsgBox function to create an alert box like that shown in Figure 11.1. A command using the MsgBox function takes the following form:

```
MsgBox(prompt[, buttons][, title])
```

The parts of this expression are as follows:

| Dialog Box Item | Meaning |
| --- | --- |
| prompt | A text string to put into the alert box. This is the message |
| buttons | An optional integer value representing the buttons to display in the dialog box, and whether to show an icon as well. The value is the sum of all the values chosen for each item—button or icon—to display. A list of the relevant values follows. If omitted, the value is assumed to be 0 |
| title | An optional text string to appear at the top of the dialog box |

Values for the buttons part of the MsgBox function are:

| Value | Meaning |
| --- | --- |
| 0 | Display OK button only |
| 1 | Display OK and Cancel buttons |
| 2 | Display Abort, Retry, and Ignore buttons |

(continues)

| Value | Meaning |
|---|---|
| 3 | Display Yes, No, and Cancel buttons |
| 4 | Display Yes and No buttons |
| 5 | Display Retry and Cancel buttons |
| 16 | Display Critical Message icon, looks like a stop sign |
| 32 | Display Warning Query icon, a question mark within a circle |
| 48 | Display Warning Message icon, an exclamation point within a circle |
| 64 | Display Information Message icon, a lower-case exclamation point within a filled circle |
| 0 | First button is default |
| 256 | Second button is default |
| 512 | Third button is default |
| 0 | Application modal; the user must respond to the message box before continuing work in the currently active application but can switch out of the application to another |
| 4096 | System modal; all applications are suspended until the user responds to the message box; user cannot switch out of the application into another |

To obtain the appropriate button combination, sum the values from the preceding table for every option you desire. Thus, to display Yes, No, and Cancel buttons and a warning message icon, add 3 to 48 to get 51, and enter that in place of *buttons*, as shown in the following code line:

```
MsgBox("Should I make the suggested change?", 51,
       "About to Ruin File")
```

You need to be able to tell which button was clicked in such a case. To determine which button was clicked, put a numeric variable into an assignment statement with the MsgBox statement, as in

```
Reply= MsgBox("Should I make the suggested change?", 51.
              "About to Ruin File")
```

The available responses are shown in the following table:

| Value Returned | Button Clicked |
| --- | --- |
| 1 | OK |
| 2 | Cancel |
| 3 | Abort |
| 4 | Retry |
| 5 | Ignore |
| 6 | Yes |
| 7 | No |

Figure 11.5 shows the results of all this in action.

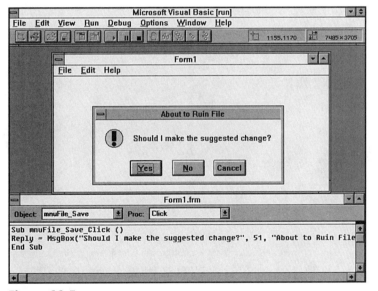

**Figure 11.5**
The alert dialog box resulting from the code shown.

## The InputBox Function

The InputBox function creates a text input dialog box. Such a dialog box lets the user type in some text, which your program presumably stores and uses someplace else. The general form of the InputBox function is:

```
TextInput=InputBox(prompt[, title][, default])
```

The parts of this expression mean the following:

| Input Box Item | Meaning |
| --- | --- |
| *TextInput* | The name of a variable into which to put the text the user enters in this dialog box |
| *prompt* | An optional text string telling the user what to enter in the text box |
| *title* | An optional text string to display across the top of the input box as a title |
| *default* | An optional text string to display in the text box as a default when the dialog box first appears. If this item is omitted, the text edit box will be blank |

For example, the statement

```
Reply=Inputbox("Enter your favorite ice cream flavor",
               "Flavor Preference", "Vanilla")
```

produces the input box shown in Figure 11.6.

**Figure 11.6**
The input dialog box, as described by the code shown in this section.

**Note** The InputBox function has an alternative version, InputBox$, which you use with string variables. The standard InputBox function works with variant type variables.

## The Common Dialog Control

A common dialog box, although the most complicated in appearance, is really the simplest to use. You need only drag its icon out on the form in which you want the dialog box to appear. There are simple commands to invoke a common dialog box when you need one. Figure 11.7 shows a common dialog command icon on Form1.

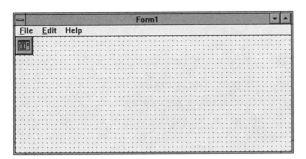

**Figure 11.7**
The common dialog tool icon.

# Activating Dialog Boxes within Code

You've seen how to activate input and message boxes at the appropriate point; you include a statement defining the dialog box, using either the MsgBox or InputBox functions. To activate the common dialog box, however, you must use the dialog's Action method, set to a numeric value equivalent to the dialog you want to display.

**Note**   Before you can use the Common Dialog control, you must install it in your project. You use the Add File command to do so. The Common Dialog control's file is named CMDIALOG.VBX; you can find it in the SYSTEM directory within your WINDOWS directory. See the last part of Lesson 13, "Additional User Input," for information on adding custom controls such as CMDIALOG.VBX to a project.

Common dialog action property values are described in the following table:

| Action Value | Meaning |
| --- | --- |
| 0 | Do nothing |
| 1 | Display the Open dialog box |
| 2 | Display the Save As dialog box |
| 3 | Display the Color dialog box |
| 4 | Display the Font dialog box |
| 5 | Display the Print Dialog box |

Thus, to show a Save dialog box within your program code, include a line like

```
CommonDialog1.Action=1
```

in the appropriate procedure. Most likely, this procedure is associated with a Save or Save As command in your application's File menu. Figure 11.8 shows a Save As dialog box called by the File menu's Save command in our running example.

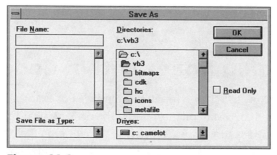

**Figure 11.8**
Invoking a Save As dialog box with the common dialog tool.

Each form of the common dialog box has properties into which the relevant choices the user makes are stored. For example, the FileName property of the Save As and Open dialog boxes contains a text string representing the name of the file chosen. These names are referenced like any property; thus, the statements

```
CommonDialog1.ShowSave
FileNameEntered = CommonDialog1.FileName
```

open a Save As dialog box. After the user clicks OK on the dialog box, the value of the name entered by the user for the file to save is put into a variable named FileNameEntered.

The FileName property is the most important property for both the Open and Save versions of the common dialog box. Before you can use this information, however, you need to know how to access the Windows file system. This information is contained in Lesson 17, "Storing, Retrieving, and Printing Data."

One more thing: Before you use the Common Dialog control, you need to set the file filters within it. You do this using the Filter property. Setting this property determines what files may be shown; the user makes the choice in the "List Files of Type" drop-down list in the dialog box. You set the Filter property with a statement of the form:

```
CMDialog1.Filter="Description1¦Filter1¦
                  Description2¦Filter2¦...
                  DescriptionLast¦FilterLast"
```

You write the filters using DOS wildcard characters and regular text. `*.TXT` specifies all files with a TXT extension. The following code sets the filters to "All Files" and "Text Files," and opens an Open version of the Common Dialog:

```
CMDialog1.Filter="All Files¦*.*¦Text Files¦*.TXT"
CMDialog1.Action=1
```

 **Tip** Check out Visual Basic's online Help for more information on using the Common Dialog control, including properties available for more esoteric functions.

# Review

In this lesson, you learned the following:

☐ Messages to the user, or requests to the user for more information, can be displayed in dialog boxes.

☐ There are three kinds of dialog boxes. An alert box displays a message, and offers a limited choice of action to the user through one or more command buttons. An input box prompts the user to enter text information. A common dialog box lets the user make choices, such as from a file or font list.

☐ Alert and input boxes are created using the MsgBox and InputBox functions, respectively.

☐ Common dialog boxes are created using the common dialog control. Only one instance of this control need be placed on each form requiring one or more common dialog boxes. The dialog box is activated within a procedure using the Action method on the Common Dialog control; the value to which this method is set determines which version of the dialog appears.

**II**

**Intermediate Topics**

 **Quiz**    Now you should be ready for the quiz.

Lesson 12

# Using Graphics

## Overview

Out of forms and controls you can craft a Visual Basic program with considerable function-ality and appeal. However, there are non-functional items that Visual Basic provides which can enhance a program and really make it shine. Through the judicious and artful use of graphics—lines, boxes, circles, and even color pictures—you can transform a powerful but plain application into a powerful and exciting one. To that end, Visual Basic provides a number of tools that enable you to create and incorporate high-quality graphics into all your application programs.

This lesson examines the following items regarding graphics in a Visual Basic program:

☐ Graphics types, including line-drawings and bitmapped graphics

☐ Graphics inserted when a program is designed, and graphics inserted when a program runs

☐ Controls for graphics

☐ Methods for graphics

☐ Drawing single points and clearing the screen

☐ Setting new coordinate units

## Graphics in Visual Basic

Before using graphics in Visual Basic, you need to understand the different types of graphics available, and how they're constructed. With such an understanding you'll be well equipped to make the appropriate decisions regarding graphics as you design your applications. One aspect of Visual Basic graphics to keep in mind is the difference between those inserted at design time, and those inserted at run time. Another critical aspect is the difference between bitmapped and object-oriented graphics.

## Types of Graphics

Once drawn on your computer screen, all graphics consist of rows and columns of colored dots. These dots are called *pixels*, a contraction of the term *picture element*. A fundamental difference in graphics lies in how these dots are stored within your computer's memory.

In a bitmapped graphic, number values represent each pixel according to some predefined formula. Thus, the entire graphic is stored as rows and columns of numbers. In an object-oriented graphic, your computer stores, in effect, a recipe for the graphic. This recipe is actually a small computer program describing how the graphic is to be drawn.

Object-oriented graphics have a major advantage over bitmapped ones: they can be made device-independent. That is, the same recipe can be used to generate graphics on different systems, and even different devices (such as on printers). What's more, the recipe for an object-oriented graphic can be scaled to the fineness—called *resolution*—of the device it's on, with one resolution when it appears on-screen and another—probably better—one when it's printed. A bitmapped graphic always has the same resolution. That means a bitmapped graphic can't take advantage of an output device with better resolution. You'll see ragged edges, or *jaggies*, on such a graphic. An object-oriented graphic output on a better device comes out smooth.

So one consideration about Visual Basic graphics is how they're stored. Another is how they're generated in the first place: at design time using graphics controls, or at run time using graphics methods.

## Graphics Controls

In Visual Basic, there are three graphics controls: the image control, the line control, and the shape control. The image control is used to bring hitmapped or object oriented images into a Visual Basic application; this can be done at either design time or run time. The line and shape controls are used to create geometrical forms at design time; in a sense these are strictly object-oriented controls.

## Graphics at Run Time

You create graphics at run time—that is, when your program's users run the program—using graphics methods. (We'll have more to say about methods in general in Lesson 14, "Methods, Procedures, and Functions.") There are several graphics methods available. Some set or return the value of a single pixel; others can be used to create objects.

## About the Coordinate System

One last thing you need to know about Visual Basic graphics is how to use the coordinate system. Hopefully, you recall something about coordinates from basic algebra. Coordinates offer a way to specify the location of something—usually a single point—by measuring its position relative to a starting point. In Visual Basic, this starting point is the upper-left corner of an object.

Two coordinates, conventionally designated $x$ and $y$, are used to indicate the position of an object. The value of the $x$ coordinate, which specifies horizontal position, ranges from 0 at the extreme left out to the maximum width of the screen. The value of the $y$ coordinate specifies vertical position, starting from 0 at the top of the screen and increasing downward.

The last thing you need to know about the coordinate system is the measurement system used. By default, Visual Basic uses what Microsoft calls twips. A *twip* is one twentieth of a printer's point, which itself is approximately equal to 1/72nd of an inch. There are, therefore, 1440 twips per inch. Thus, a coordinate location exactly two inches to the right of, and one inch below, the top corner is referenced as (2880, 1440) in the Visual Basic coordinate system.

 **Note**   It is possible to use a different scale for any object's coordinate system, to specify measurements in inches, points, and the like. See the section "Changing Coordinate Units" at the end of this lesson.

With these preliminaries out of the way, we're ready to learn how to use graphics in Visual Basic.

# Using Graphics Controls

To repeat, there are three basic graphics controls: the shape control, the image control, and the line control. Figure 12.1 shows objects drawn with each of these three controls.

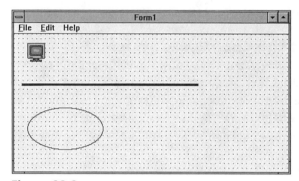

**Figure 12.1**
A bitmapped image, a line, and a shape.

Remember the following points about graphics controls:

☐ Generally speaking, graphics controls cannot contain other controls.

☐ Graphics controls cannot appear on top of another control, unless they themselves are contained by that control or within a frame.

☐ Graphics controls accept event procedures as other controls do. For example, you can use the image control as a button, which the user can then click to perform an action. Part of that action might be to change the appearance of the image control itself, providing feedback to the user.

## The Image Control

The image control enables you to drag out a frame into which a picture may be loaded. This picture can be either a bitmapped or object-oriented graphic. Further, the picture can be loaded either at design time, or when the program runs. Figure 12.2 shows some filled image controls on a form.

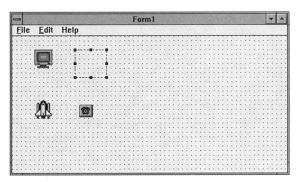

**Figure 12.2**
Four image controls, three of which contain pictures.

Take the following steps to create and load an image control:

1. Click to select the image control on the toolbox.

2. Drag out the image outline on the form on which you want it to appear.

3. With the image outline selected, access the Properties window.

4. Select the Picture property, and double-click the ellipsis at the top of the Properties window.

5. Using the dialog box that appears, choose an image to put into the image control.

You don't have to load a specific picture when you first create an image control; you actually can have your Visual Basic program do this for you when the program is run. Doing so enables you to have more than one picture appear within the control, depending perhaps on some action the user performs. You might have one of several pictures load according to which button a user clicks, for example. In this way you offer the user visual feedback.

You use the LoadPicture function (more information on functions is found in Lesson 13, "Additional User Input") to put a graphic into an image control at run time, using the image's Picture property. You also can use this function to replace a graphic previously loaded, even at design time. Thus, the statement:

```
Image1.Picture = LoadPicture("C:\MYAPP\PICTURE.BMP")
```

loads a bitmapped graphic named PICTURE (found in the MYAPP directory on drive C) into the image control named Image1.

**Caution**

Keep in mind, however, that to load pictures at run time, the pictures must be present in the correct location on the computer running the program. If your Visual Basic program can't find the appropriate picture on the computer running the program, it will display an error message and stop running. Pictures loaded at design time, on the other hand, become part of your Visual Basic application, and don't have to be provided separately.

The image control will accept four different types of graphics files, each distinguished by a unique file extension. These files are described in the following table:

| Format | Description |
| --- | --- |
| .BMP | Windows bitmap files. Such files are produced by, among other applications, Windows Paintbrush, one of the Windows Accessories |
| .DIB | An alternative bitmap file format |
| .ICO | Windows icon files. These are special bitmap files, measuring 32x32 pixels, generally used to provide icons for use within the Windows Program Manager |
| .WMF | Windows MetaFiles. These are object-oriented graphics files. Only files created in Windows 3.0 or later can be used in Visual Basic |

**Note**

There is no way to create any of these graphics in Visual Basic itself. You have to rely on some form of graphics software (such as Windows Paintbrush) to create the graphics outside of Visual Basic. There are a number of very reasonably priced tools for this kind of thing available as shareware on CompuServe and America Online, among other places.

## The Line Control

The image control is useful for complex graphics, but for merely dressing up your application, it may be overkill. Visual Basic has other controls for creating simple graphic elements at design time, perhaps the simplest of which is the straight line.

Use the line control to draw straight lines on a form. Figure 12.3 shows several lines drawn on an otherwise blank form.

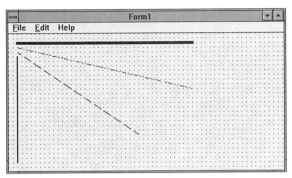

**Figure 12.3**
Four lines of various styles, thicknesses, and angles.

Using the BorderColor, BorderStyle, and BorderWidth properties of a line control object, you can set the color and thickness of a line, and also set whether the line should be solid or dashed. Drag the end points on the line object itself to adjust its length.

Follow these steps to create a line and adjust its properties:

1. Click to select the line control on the toolbox.

2. Click and drag out a line on the desired form.

   The line may be in any position: vertical, horizontal, or diagonal.

3. Press F4 with the line selected to bring up the Properties window.

4. Enter the desired values. The BorderWidth property sets the line width; enter a width in pixels.

One handy way in which to use lines is to divide a frame into separate areas. Just drag a line out across the area you want to divide.

## The Shape Control

Although you can use lines to create boxes and other shapes, there's a less cumbersome way to do so: use the Shape control. This control also enables you to create circles and ovals, something you can't do with straight lines. Several shape control examples are shown in Figure 12.4.

II

Intermediate Topics

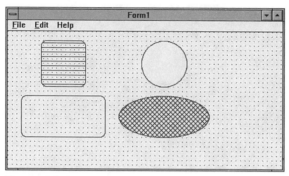

**Figure 12.4**
Geometric figures drawn with the Shape control.

There are four fundamental figures available, two of which appear in variant forms with rounded corners. Figures available are rectangles (with either sharp or rounded corners), squares (also with either sharp or rounded corners), circles, and ovals (also called ellipses).

As with lines, you can set a number of appearance properties for these figures, including the color of the outline or the interior, a pattern to use when filling, and whether it is possible to see through the figure. Use the BorderColor, BackColor, FillStyle, and BackStyle properties, respectively, to adjust these attributes.

Follow these steps to create a figure and adjust its properties:

1. Click to select the shape control on the toolbox.

2. Drag out a bounding rectangle for the desired shape on the appropriate form.

   This rectangle is an outline within which the desired figure will fit. The rectangle itself does not appear at run time; it only serves as a boundary for the figure you're creating.

3. Press F4 with the boundary rectangle selected to access the Properties window.

4. Click the Shape property, then choose from the drop-down menu at the top of the Properties window to select the shape to use.

5. Enter values for other properties you want to set.

Once you've selected a shape, you can adjust its size and position using the sizing handles that appear upon it whenever you click to select it. As with all object properties, you can change shape properties at run time with the appropriate assignment statements. This enables you, among other things, to change the width or color of a shape as your program runs.

# Drawing at Run Time: Graphics Methods

You've now seen how to add graphics, or at least placeholders for graphics, when you design an application. You also can insert Visual Basic programming code into an application that will draw graphics for you directly when a program is run, as you'll see in this section.

Visual Basic has a number of statements, called graphics methods, which you use to have your program create simple geometrical forms. These statements include methods to control the appearance of the screen, allowing you, for example, to erase it prior to starting a new graphic. Figure 12.5 shows graphics created using methods.

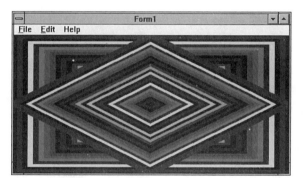

**Figure 12.5**
Some results of using graphics methods.

Exactly what are methods? As mentioned earlier, you'll learn more about the concept of methods in Visual Basic in Lesson 14, "Methods, Procedures, and Functions." For now, you can think of a method as a small, pre-defined program to do one specific task. In the case of graphics methods, this task is to create something on-screen out of pixels. Visual Basic graphics methods include:

Intermediate Topics

| Method | Action |
| --- | --- |
| Cls | Clear the screen |
| Circle | Draw a circle or oval |
| Line | Draw a line or box |
| Point | Find out what color value a specified point has |
| Pset | Set a specified point to a given color |

Why use methods? There are a couple of reasons. For one thing, the Pset method is the only way you can draw a single pixel or a pattern of pixels. In addition, you may find that certain graphics applications—especially ones involving lots of repetition—are easier to create with a few lines of programming code, rather than using a large number of graphics controls. This advantage increases if you're creating graphics that need to fit a boundary whose size the user may set. Consider, for example, lines within a pie chart whose size the user might change.

Because methods are statements, they appear in procedures. You must, therefore, make sure your graphics routines written with methods appear in the correct procedure. For example, if you want a graphic to appear whenever a form is displayed, you must put the correct methods into the Paint event for that form; putting them into the Load event won't work.

**Caution** Graphics methods can be more resource-intensive than graphics controls, meaning they can slow down your application. They also are harder to get "just right." With controls, you can see the effects of small tweaks as you perform them. With methods, you have to run the program to check the results of changes, which takes more time and effort.

## Drawing Lines

Use the Line method to create simple lines and polygons (for example, triangles, squares, and rectangles). Figure 12.6 shows several figures created using the Line method.

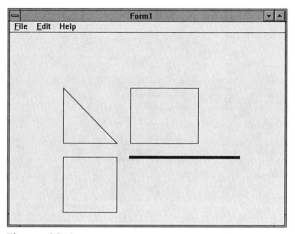

**Figure 12.6**
A triangle, square, rectangle, and thick line created using the Line method.

A statement using the Line method takes the following form:

```
[objectname.]Line[(starting coordinates)]
              -(ending coordinates) [,color][,B][F]
```

Parts of the statement within brackets are optional. Note the letters B and F. Using B causes Visual Basic to draw a box whose upper left corner is at the first pair of coordinates in the line statement. The box's lower right corner appears at the second set of coordinates. Using F with B fills the box with the current fill pattern and color, set using the FillStyle, FillColor, and BackColor properties for the object on which you're drawing. The statement

```
Form1.Line (0,0) - (1440, 1440),,B
```

draws a square on Form1, starting at the upper-left corner. Note that the coordinate values can be given using variables or expressions, enabling you to create general procedures for drawing objects whose exact placement and appearance depends on variable contents or expression values, as in:

```
Form1.Line (Startx,Starty) - ((Startx + Run), (Starty + Rise))
```

You can omit the object designation if you want the graphic to appear on the current form. You also can omit the starting coordinates if you want the line to take off from the current graphics point. If no graphics have yet been drawn, the current point is (0,0). If graphics have been drawn, the current point is the last one specified. For example, if the preceding statement is run, the current point becomes (1440,1440). You can take advantage of this to draw closed polygons. Figure 12.7 shows the code used to draw the triangle shown in Figure 12.6.

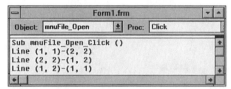

```
Form1.frm
Object: mnuFile_Open    Proc: Click
Sub mnuFile_Open_Click ()
Line (1, 1)-(2, 2)
Line (2, 2)-(1, 2)
Line (1, 2)-(1, 1)
```

**Figure 12.7**
Visual Basic code using the Line method to create a triangle.

When you want to draw closed graphics, you can specify coordinates relative to the last point drawn, rather than relative to the upper-left corner of the object on which you're drawing. It's like saying, "From here, draw a line segment down to this relative position." You do this using the Step keyword, as in

```
Line (1440, 1440)-Step (2880,0)
```

This statement starts at a point two inches down and across from the form's upper left corner. It then draws a two-inch horizontal line; the Step keyword makes the second set of coordinates relative to the first. If the Step keyword had been omitted, the line drawn would have been one inch long, not two.

## Drawing Curves

Use the Circle method to draw circles, ovals, and arcs (sections of circles) on the desired object. Figure 12.8 shows an example of each such graphic.

A statement using the Circle method takes this form:

```
[objectname.]Circle [Step](x,y)radius[,color]
```

objectname specifies the object on which the circle is to be drawn; it may be omitted if the circle is to be drawn on the current form. x and y specify the coordinate location of the circle's center, radius specifies its size. The Step keyword is optional, and specifies a center location relative to the current point, rather than one given in absolute terms. Thus, the statement

```
Circle (2880,2880) 1440
```

draws a circle with a one-inch radius at a location two inches down and two inches across from the upper-left corner of the current form.

**Figure 12.8**
A circle, an ellipse, and an arc drawn using the `Circle` method.

To draw an arc or an ellipse, you must include start and end values for the arc, and an aspect ratio (width to height) for an ellipse. Start and end values are angles expressed in radians. In an ellipse, the start and end values may be omitted, but commas must be used as placeholders. Figure 12.9 shows the code used to create the arc and the ellipse shown in Figure 12.8.

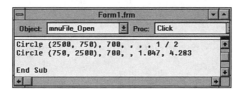

**Figure 12.9**
Code used to create the arc and ellipse shown.

## Screen Maintenance
To draw a single point on the current object, use the `Pset` method. Figure 12.10 shows several points drawn using this method, along with the code to draw them.

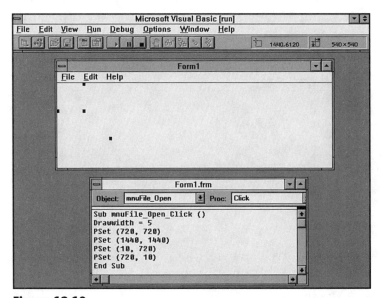

**Figure 12.10**
Points drawn on a form, with the Visual Basic code that created them.

The PSet method takes the form

```
[Objectname.]PSet (x,y)[,color]
```

If *Objectname* is omitted, the point is drawn on the current form. *x* and *y* specify the coordinate location of the point to be drawn. If you omit *color*, the point is set to the object's current foreground color. The statement

```
Pset (1440,1440)
```

draws a single point one inch down and one inch across from the top left corner on the current form.

Finally, use the Cls statement to clear out the specified drawing area, removing all graphics (if any) heretofore placed on it. The statement takes the general form:

```
[objectname.]Cls
```

If *objectname* is omitted, Visual Basic clears the current form.

# Changing Coordinate Units

At the beginning of this lesson, you learned that Visual Basic uses a default coordinate system in which measurements are given relative to the upper left corner in units of twips, where one twip is 1/1440th of an inch. You do not have to restrict yourself to this scale if you don't want to. Using the ScaleMode property, you can choose new units for any object, including individual controls or an entire form.

Visual Basic supports the following scale modes:

| ScaleMode Setting | Units |
| --- | --- |
| 0 | User-defined |
| 1 | Twips |
| 2 | Points |
| 3 | Pixels |
| 4 | Characters (also known as Picas) |
| 5 | Inches |
| 6 | Millimeters |
| 7 | Centimeters |

To set the scale for Form1 to measure in inches, for example, use the following statement:

```
Form1.ScaleMode=5
```

# Review

In this lesson, you learned the following:

☐ There are two basic graphics types: line drawings and bitmapped graphics. Bitmapped graphics are stored as a sequence of numbers, each representing a single pixel. Line drawings, also known as object-oriented graphics, consist of sequences of statements telling the computer how and where to draw graphics elements.

☐ Use graphics controls to insert graphics as a program is designed. These controls include: the image control, used to insert bitmapped or object-oriented graphics; the line control, used to create straight lines; and the shape control, used to create circles, ovals, rectangles, and squares.

☐ Use graphics methods to draw objects directly on-screen when a program is run. The `Line` method draws lines and polygons; the `Circle` method draws circles, ovals, and arcs; the `Pset` method draws a single point on the screen; and the `Cls` method clears anything that has been drawn on-screen.

☐ Use the `ScaleMode` property of an object to change coordinate units for that object.

Now you should be ready for the quiz.

## Lesson 13

# Additional User Input

## Overview

In this lesson we summarize additional ways to add functionality to a Visual Basic program through its user interface. You'll learn more about the different kinds of control buttons offered in Visual Basic. Most of these should be quite familiar to you if you have any experience at all in working with Microsoft Windows applications. In the following pages you'll see how to harness them for your own purposes.

This lesson covers the following points regarding getting user input in a Visual Basic program:

☐ The different types of buttons available

☐ Mutually exclusive and multiple choices using option and checkbox buttons

☐ Text input with text, list, and combo boxes

☐ Adding custom controls

## More Ways of Communicating with the Application User

A good computer application always presents a range of choices to the user. Think of word processing software, in which you can choose the font and style in which to present text, the line spacing to use when printing it, and so on. While the value of presenting choices ought to be clear, the different ways in which you might do so probably aren't. We hope to rectify that here.

First, the way in which choices are presented depends on what kind of information is needed from the user. Think of an application again. If the choice is whether or not to take some action, a command button can be used to solicit user input; although if the choices are mutually exclusive, some other type of button might be better. If the program requires text input from the user at some point, then a way for the user to enter that text must be presented. To save the user time in cases where standard choices are available, you might want to list these choices near the text box and allow the user to select from them. Again, it all depends on what your program needs at any point.

The kinds of choice mechanisms we're discussing appear to break down into two broad categories: those that ask for some sort of user decision—what to do or use, and what not to—and those that require text input. The former can be handled using buttons, and the latter can be handled by text, list, and combo boxes.

## Buttons

Visual Basic offers three different kinds of buttons (one is actually called a "box," but it's still something the user clicks) geared to different needs. Figure 13.1 shows a form with examples of each button type.

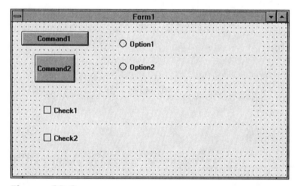

**Figure 13.1**
Command and option buttons, and checkboxes.

Command boxes enable the program user to initiate an action; a specific procedure is executed when the user clicks such a button. Option buttons and checkboxes are slightly different. Option buttons require the user to select from among mutually exclusive options; for example, the user might select what style in which to present text. Checkboxes are used for the same sort of choices in cases where the options aren't mutually exclusive; the user can check one, all, or any combination of the checkbox options presented. While there may be procedures associated with clicking either option buttons or checkboxes, there don't have to be. In many cases, some other procedure will check the status of such options (selected or unselected) before determining exactly how to execute.

## Text, List, and Combo Boxes

Visual Basic offers three different ways for an application user to select or enter text information. Figure 13.2 shows a form with examples of each text entry option.

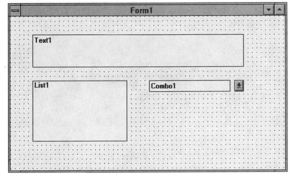

**Figure 13.2**
Text, list, and combo boxes.

Using a text entry box, a user can type in any desired combination of characters, up to the maximum capacity of the box, which is set at design time by way of a property, MaxLength. A list box lets the user choose from among several predetermined options; a particular option may or may not be highlighted as a default choice. A combo box does as its name implies; it combines the functions of a text entry box and a list box, enabling the user to either select a predetermined option or type in a different one.

## Custom Controls

In addition to the options previously discussed, Visual Basic allows you to add any of several custom controls to your application. The exact custom controls available to you will depend on the version of Visual Basic you're using; The Professional Edition has more custom controls. Figure 13.3 shows a form with a few custom controls on it, including some of the fancy buttons that are part of THREED.VBX, an animated button from ANIBUTTON.VBX, and a grid control example from GRID.VBX.

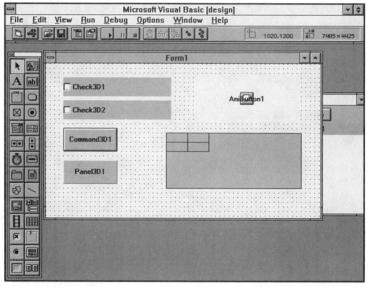

**Figure 13.3**
Custom controls: 3-D and animated buttons, and the grid control; note the eight additional control icons at the bottom of the toolbox used to create these custom controls.

You'll learn exactly how to add custom controls to an application in the final part of this lesson.

# Using Buttons

As with just about all Visual Basic controls, there are two parts to enabling a particular control button. First, you must create the button, setting its properties in the process. Second, you must write programming code to take advantage of the button's presence, defining what happens when the user clicks that particular button. The way in which you do these things depends on which button you want to define.

## Command Button Control

We've demonstrated command buttons in several previous lessons. These buttons are designed to perform a specific action whenever the user clicks them. Figure 13.4 shows a form with several command buttons, along with the programming code associated with them.

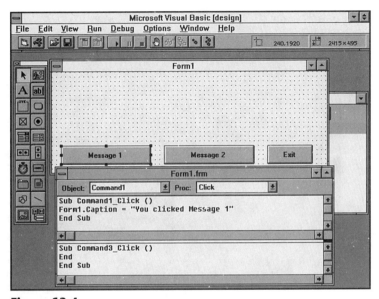

**Figure 13.4**
Three command buttons, along with code for two of them.

Take the following steps to define a command button:

1. Click the command button icon on the toolbox.

2. Click and drag out the button on the appropriate form.

3. With the button selected, press F4 to bring up the Properties window. Set properties for the button, including its name and whether it has a caption. Click to close the Properties window.

4. Double-click the button to open the Code window. Type in the appropriate programming code to define what happens when the user clicks the button.

## Option Button Control

Option buttons differ from command buttons, and not just in the way they look. For one thing, they always appear in groups. For another thing, the user may choose only one such option from any group of option buttons.

Finally, nothing necessarily happens the moment a user clicks a given option button, other than it suddenly appears filled in with a dot to show it's been selected. Other parts of your application may check the status of the button when they execute, to determine what to do. It's possible, of course, to write a Click procedure for an option button; if for example you'd like other buttons to be enabled or disabled when the user clicks a specific option. Figure 13.5 shows a group of option buttons on a form.

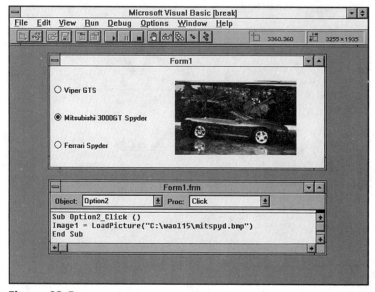

**Figure 13.5**
Three option buttons, used to choose which picture to display in the image control to the right; choices made with option buttons are mutually exclusive.

There are some things you need to know about option buttons before you proceed:

☐ Option buttons always appear in groups. Only one button in a group may be selected; selecting one deselects another.

☐ All option buttons on a form are considered part of a single group *unless* the buttons appear within frames. To have two groups on one form, you must have two frames, in which each separate group of buttons appears.

☐ To have one particular button within a group appear selected as the default choice, set its Value property to True.

You also should know that certain option button properties govern how each button appears on-screen. The `Alignment` property, for example, governs whether the button appears to the right or the left of the caption. The `Caption` property, of course, should be set a brief description of what choice the button is all about. Read about other control properties in Lesson 5, "About Controls."

Take these steps to define a group of option buttons within a frame:

1. Click the frame tool icon on the toolbox. Click and drag out a frame on the appropriate form.

2. Click the option button tool icon on the toolbox. Click and drag out an option button within the frame. Repeat until the required number of buttons have been created.

3. With the first option button selected, press F4 to access the Properties window. Give the button a caption defining it to the user. Choose other properties as appropriate. Repeat for the other buttons in the group, and to give an appropriate caption to the frame. Set the `Value` property to True for the button you want to represent the default choice, if any.

4. If you want some action to be performed as soon as a given button is clicked, double-click it to open the code window. Enter programming code as appropriate to define a procedure for what happens when the button is clicked.

If some other part of your application needs to know which option in a group has been selected, you need some way of determining which one the user clicked. You could do so using `If...Then` statements to check the `Value` property of each button, as in

```
If Option1.Value = True Then
    statements
End If
If Option2.Value = True Then
    statements
End If
```

For any group of option buttons, only one will have a `Value` of True; the rest will be False. Remember that, if you don't set a default choice at design time by giving one option the value True, then, if the user never clicks one, it might happen that none of them will be True when the appropriate part of your program executes. This will crash your program if it expects a choice to be made. It's therefore a good idea *always* to provide a default choice.

## Checkbox Control

Checkboxes let you present the user with one or more options that are independent of each other. The user may select one, all, or any combination of such options. Unlike option buttons, checkboxes do not form groups as far as Visual Basic is concerned. You are free, of course, to think of a particular set of boxes as a group if you want; it makes no difference to the operation of the program. Figure 13.6 shows such a group of checkboxes on a form.

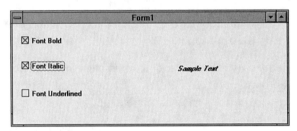

**Figure 13.6**
Three checkboxes to control the way a label displays text; two of the boxes are checked, to show how the effects of a group of checkboxes can be cumulative.

Some things to know about checkboxes:

☐ You can set alignment for checkboxes as you can for option buttons; this determines whether the box appears to the left or right of the caption.

☐ If at some point in your application a particular choice becomes temporarily invalid, you can disable the relevant checkbox by setting its Value property to 2 (Dimmed).

☐ To have a button appear selected as a default choice, set its Value property to 1.

A checkbox that has been selected has an X in its box; otherwise, the box is blank. Clicking a selected box deselects it, getting rid of the X. In short, clicking a checkbox switches its value to the opposite setting.

Take these steps to define checkboxes on a form:

1. Click the checkbox tool icon on the toolbox.

2. Click and drag out a checkbox on the appropriate form. Repeat for each checkbox you want to define.

3. With a checkbox selected, press F4 to access the Properties window. Set the desired properties, repeating for each checkbox.

   Be sure to set each `Caption` property to appropriately label the box.

   If you want something to happen as soon as the user clicks a given box, you must define a procedure for it in the Click event.

4. Double-click the box to access the Code window. Enter the appropriate code to define the procedure for what happens when a user clicks the box.

As with option buttons, you don't have to define a procedure for what happens as soon as the user clicks a box; some other procedure within your program may instead check a box's status at the appropriate point. Unlike the case of a group of option buttons, it's perfectly reasonable for no checkboxes to have been selected. Code to check the status of a particular checkbox might look like:

```
If Check1.Value = 1 Then
    statements
End If
```

# Accepting Text Input

Buttons present predefined choices to a user, but there are times when an application may require information whose exact form cannot be anticipated. The user's name and address, entered the first time a program is run to personalize it (and discourage pirate copies), is one example. Visual Basic offers several ways to allow a user to enter text at the appropriate point within a program. The simplest of these is the text box control.

## The Text Box Control

Using the text box control, you can create one or more framed areas into which a user may type text. Figure 13.7 shows a text box on a form.

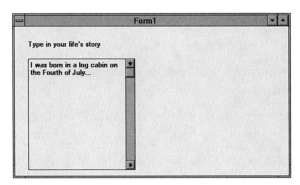

**Figure 13.7**
Giving the user a place to enter text; notice the vertical scroll bar at the text box's right.

Here's a summary of important points about text boxes:

☐ A text box will support only one line of text unless its MultiLine property is set to True.

☐ Within a multiline text box, you may set the ScrollBars property to True to display scroll bars, with which the user can move text up and down to see past what will fit within the box.

These scroll bars are not the same as the scroll bars tool.

☐ You may set a maximum length for text entered into a text box using the MaxLength property.

☐ Text entered within a text box is stored in the box's value. The value of a text box is, appropriately enough, its Text property. To retrieve text from a text box, use a statement like:

```
TextHolderVariable=TextBox1.Text
```

Follow this procedure to create a text box on a form:

1. Click to select the text box tool on the toolbox.

2. Click and drag out a text box on the appropriate form.

3. With the text box selected, press F4 to bring up the Properties window. Set properties as desired, including the MultiLine, ScrollBars, and MaxLength properties. Delete the text in the Text property to keep the box from displaying its default name; alternatively you may want to enter default text for the box to display.

Generally speaking, you don't define event procedures for text boxes. How to dispose of the text a user enters is left up to some other part of the program. For example, to enable a limited form of password protection, you can have a procedure compare the contents of a text box with a predetermined value, and then use the results elsewhere in a program. The following few lines of code check the text entered by the user in a text box named PassWordBox, and compare the contents to a known text string. The variable *Verified* is assumed to be a global variable, whose contents can thus be checked by other procedures.

```
If PassWordBox.Text = "Password" Then
        Verified = True
Else
        Verified = False
End If
```

**Tip** Use the PasswordChar property to protect the privacy of password text boxes at run time. Set this property to display a specific character (usually an asterisk).

## List Boxes

Should you want to limit a user's text entry choices to a set list, rather than allowing them to enter almost anything, you easily can do so using—you guessed it—the list box control. A list box does just that: present a list of text choices to the user. Figure 13.8 shows a form with two list boxes.

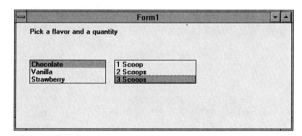

**Figure 13.8**
Giving the user text choices with two list boxes.

Creating list boxes is a little bit more involved than merely dragging out text boxes. You see, you have to get the choices into the list. This is done using the AddItem method.

The general form of an AddItem statement to put a choice into a list box is:

`ListName.AddItem TextExpression[,index]`

`ListName` is the name of the list box to which you're adding an item; `TextExpression` is either a string variable or constant. `Index` is the position in the list at which to add the item; the first position is 0. Thus, to add the choice "United States" to the beginning of a list box named `ListCountries`, you'd use the line

`ListCountries.AddItem "United States",0`

All such statements should appear in the `Form_Load` procedure of the form on which the list box appears *unless* some other part of your program needs to modify the list (based on something the user did); in that case, relevant statements should go in that part of the program.

If you want the items in your list to appear in alphabetical order, you can let Visual Basic do the work for you. Omit the index, and set the Sorted property to True.

Figure 13.9 shows the code used to fill the list boxes shown in Figure 13.8.

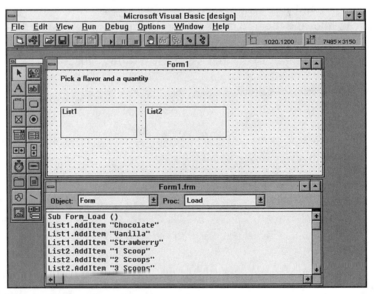

**Figure 13.9**
Adding items to two list boxes.

Follow these steps to create a list box on a form:

1. Click to select the list box tool on the toolbox.

2. Click and drag out a list box on the appropriate form.

3. With the list box selected, press F4 to access the Properties window. Set properties for the box as desired, including whether the box is Sorted or not. Close the Properties window.

4. Define items for the list box. To have the items defined when the relevant form is first loaded, double-click the form to access the Form_Load event procedure. Write code to add items to the list box using the AddItem method—one line per item.

You may want to write a procedure for the DblClick event for an item on a list box. This procedure should do the same thing as the OK (or whatever other) button you have on the form to execute an action once the user has made a choice. The choice made by the user from a list box is stored in the box's Text property. Access this property in an assignment statement to retrieve the choice made.

## Combo Boxes

Should you want to give a user more flexibility, you can combine the functions of both text and list boxes. The combo box tool allows you to create combination list/text entry boxes, in which the user may select a predefined item, or type something new. Figure 13.10 shows the three types of combo boxes.

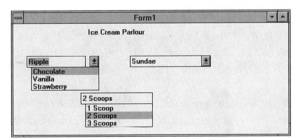

**Figure 13.10**
Three combo boxes on a form, each of a different style.

Here are a few things to know about combo boxes:

☐ As Figure 13.10 shows, there are three styles of combo boxes; you set which one you want using the Style property.

*Style 0* is a drop-down combo box; the choice list drops down when the user clicks the box. The box showing flavors in Figure 13.10 is this style of combo box.

*Style 1* is a fixed combo box; the list is always visible. The box showing number of scoops in Figure 13.10 is this style of combo box.

*Style 2* is actually a drop-down type of list box; no text entry is possible with this style. The box showing "Sundae" in Figure 13.10 is this style of combo box.

☐ As with list boxes, you add items to a combo box using the `AddItem` method.

☐ The choice the user makes is stored in the combo box's `Text` property.

Follow these steps to create a combo box on a form:

1. Click to select the combo box tool on the toolbox.

2. Click and drag out a combo box on the appropriate form.

3. With the combo box selected, press F4 to access the Properties window. Set properties for the box as desired, starting with the Style of combo box to use. Close the Properties window.

4. Define items for the combo box. To have the items defined when the relevant form is first loaded, double-click the form to access the `Form_Load` event procedure. Write code to add items to the combo box using the `AddItem` method; one line per item.

You may want to write a procedure for the `DblClick` event for an item on a combo box. This procedure should do the same thing as the OK (or whatever other) button you have on the form to execute an action once the user has made a choice. The easiest way to do this is to simply have the procedure call the appropriate command button click procedure, using the `Call` statement with the name of the command button click procedure, as in:

```
Sub ComboBox1_DblClick ()
    Call CommandOK_Click
End Sub
```

# About Custom Controls

Finally, you don't have to restrict the tools you use in an application to the standard ones you've seen so far. Visual Basic offers custom controls for you to use, depending on the version of the program you purchased (the Professional Edition has more tools). There are tools available also from third-party developers—companies other than Microsoft, the manufacturer of the base product. Incorporating any of these tools into a Visual Basic project is not difficult.

## Available Custom Controls

In the standard version of Visual Basic, there are three custom controls: the grid control, the common dialog control, and the OLE (Object Linking and Embedding) control. Each control is stored within a separate file with the extension .VBX. The grid control is named GRID.VBX, the common dialog control is named CMDIALOG.VBX, and the OLE control is named MSOLE2.VBX.

The Professional Edition of Visual Basic has many more custom controls available. These tools are beyond the scope of this book, but you can read about them in the documentation that comes with the Professional Edition. All custom controls, no matter who developed them, are stored in separate files with the .VBX extension.

## Incorporating a Custom Control into a Project

Before you can use a custom control, you must incorporate its file into your project. You do this using the Add File command in the Visual Basic File menu. Note that you can use the Remove File command to delete a custom control from a project.

Take these steps to add a custom control to a project:

1. With the project window open, choose Add File from the Visual Basic File menu.

   The Add File dialog box appears.

2. Navigate in the scrolling list until you find the name of the control you want to add. Click to select it.

3. Click OK to add the control; this also closes the Add File dialog box. An icon for the newly added control appears at the bottom of the toolbox.

4. If you want to use the new control right away, click to select the control, then drag out an instance of it on the appropriate form.

The custom dialog control was discussed in Lesson 11, "About Dialog Boxes." You can learn more about the OLE control in Lesson 18, "Communicating with Other Programs."

# Review

In this lesson, we talked about the following:

☐ There are three different types of buttons available: command buttons, option buttons, and checkbox buttons.

☐ You let the user make mutually exclusive choices using Option buttons. Only one option button within a group can be selected.

☐ You let the user make multiple choices using checkboxes. Any combination of these may be clicked; they do not exist in groups as such.

☐ The user may input text with text, list, and combo boxes.

☐ A simple text box merely provides an area in which the user types information. Its contents are stored in its Text property.

☐ A list box presents a predefined set of choices to the user. These choices are put into the list at design time using the AddItem method.

☐ A combo box combines the functions of a text input box and a list box. There are three styles of combo box; some have a drop-down list while others have lists that are always visible.

☐ Visual Basic supports the use of custom controls, each of which is stored in a separate file with the extension .VBX. You add custom controls to a project using the Add File command.

**Quiz**     Now you should be ready for the quiz.

Lesson 14

# Methods, Procedures, and Functions

## Overview

Buttons, dialog boxes, and graphics may be what the user sees, but it is within procedures that the real work of an application gets done. Procedures are something the user never sees; however, you, as a programmer, will spend much of your time there. Elsewhere in this Tutor, we've defined a procedure as a sequence of Visual Basic programming language statements, a sequence that performs some specific task. In this lesson, we'll take another look at procedures, including special-case and predefined procedures such as methods and functions.

This lesson covers the following points regarding methods, procedures, and functions in a Visual Basic program:

☐ How program tasks are accomplished in Visual Basic

☐ Different methods available for use with objects

☐ How to define procedures, and how to reference them within other parts of a program

☐ What functions are, and how to create them

☐ Predefined functions available in Visual Basic

# Getting Things Done

In other lessons, you've seen how to create event procedures; these are lists of steps to perform when a specific thing happens to a specific object, such as when the user clicks a command button. Actually, procedures are not limited to specific events. Nor do you necessarily have to write several lines of code to accomplish a task. There are three ways to get tasks done in Visual Basic.

## Object Methods

One of the simplest things you can do in Visual Basic is make some change to an object—for example, making a control invisible. While you might write a couple of lines of programming code to handle such an occurrence, there may be an even easier way. Visual Basic provides a number of methods that perform specific actions on objects.

Think of a method as a named and predefined procedure for performing a limited action on an object. For example, the `Hide` method makes an object invisible; using the `Hide` method is equivalent to setting the object's `Visible` property to False. You invoke the `Hide` method—or any method—by adding its name to the object you want to change, separated by a period. Thus,

```
Form1.Hide
```

performs the `Hide` method on `Form1`. It's the same as entering

```
Form1.Visible = False
```

You can see, though, that using the method is at least easier to type. Other methods, such as the `Move` method, save even more typing.

## Procedures

You've encountered event procedures in several previous lessons. Any procedure has a name and a body of Visual Basic programming statements. Figure 14.1 shows two procedures within the Code window; these procedures make use of methods as well.

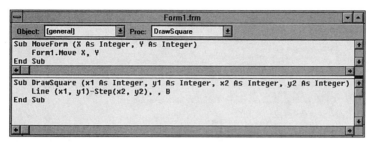

**Figure 14.1**
Two procedure definitions.

Although many procedures are invoked on certain objects after specific events, it's possible to execute a procedure from some other place within a program. In fact, you can write a single, general procedure that's run—or called—from many places within a program, involving different data each time. In this way, you harness the real power of procedures.

## Functions

A function is an example of a general procedure that may be called from any place within a program. A function, however, provides—we say *returns*—a single value after it's performed, no matter how many items of data it's provided. You've actually seen functions in other lessons, particularly when we talked about string variables. You can define your own functions, or you can use any of the number of predefined functions that are built into Visual Basic.

So there are several ways to perform programming tasks in Visual Basic. Now it's time to take a closer look. We'll start at the beginning, with methods.

# Using Object Methods

A *method* is a named procedure for performing an action on an object. Figure 14.2 shows code that uses the Move method on a command button.

**II**

**Intermediate Topics**

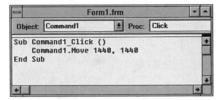

**Figure 14.2**
Using the Move method to shift a control location.

 The following is a list of the more commonly used methods. Note that not all methods work with every object. If you try to use a method on an object that doesn't support it, you'll get an error message.

| Method | Description |
|--------|-------------|
| AddItem | Add text item to specified list or combo box.<br>[*listname.*]AddItem *textexpression*[,*index*] |
| Arrange | Set arrangement of child forms within MDI form.<br>*mdiform*.Arrange *arrangement* |
| Circle | Draw circle on object with specified center and radius.<br>[*objectname.*]Circle [Step](*centerX*,<br>*centerY*),*radius*,[,[*color*][,[*start*][,*end*][,*aspect*]]]] |
| Clear | Clear contents of list or combo box.<br>*boxname*.Clear |
| Cls | Clear run-time generated graphics off object.<br>*objectname*.Cls |
| Hide | Make form invisible; same as setting Visible property to False.<br>*formname*.Hide |
| Line | Drawn line on object using endpoints specified.<br>*objectname*.Line [Step](*BeginX*,*BeginY*) -<br>[Step](*EndX*,*EndY*) |
| Move | Change position and/or size of object.<br>*objectname*.Move<br>*leftposition*[,*topposition*[,*newwidth*[,*newheight*]]] |
| NewPage | End current print page and advance to next.<br>Printer.NewPage |
| Point | Returns RGB color of a point on an object.<br>*objectname*.Point(*Xposition*,*Yposition*) |
| Print | Print text on an object.<br>*objectname*.Print *expression* |

| Method | Description |
|--------|-------------|
| PrintForm | Print form on current printer (non-MDI only).<br>*formname*.PrintForm |
| RemoveItem | Removes item from list or combo box.<br>*List1*.RemoveItem *List1*.ListIndex |
| Show | Display form.<br>*formname*.Show |

Methods, of course, don't exist in a vacuum. In fact, you can't use methods at all unless you put them within another important Visual Basic programming structure: procedures.

# Using Procedures

Whereas formerly a computer program might have contained a single mass of statements, modern practice dictates that programs be broken into discrete, easy-to-understand operations. In Visual Basic, these operations occur within procedures, which are the backbone of a Visual Basic application program. Figure 14.3 shows two short procedures in the Code window.

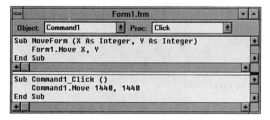

**Figure 14.3**
Two procedures that both rely on methods.

As we've said many times before, a procedure is simply a set sequence of programming language instructions, designed to perform a specific task on specific data.

## Creating Procedures

You've seen in previous lessons how simple it can be to create an event procedure for an object. You just double-click the object to open the code window and write your procedure. Event procedures, however, are not the only game in town. You also can write general procedures that any part of your program can use to perform tasks. There are several distinct steps to creating such a procedure: defining it, deciding on its scope, assigning arguments, and finally writing the actual code.

### Procedure Definitions

To create a procedure, all you have to do is tell Visual Basic to do so, and give the procedure a name. You do this using the Sub keyword and a name for the procedure:

```
Sub procedurename ()
        statements
End Sub
```

Take note of the parentheses at the end of this statement, which have to be there. In some cases, the parentheses will be filled with variable names through which a procedure acquires data from the outside world. We'll look at that in more detail shortly. The statement End Sub must appear at the end of a procedure. Between these two lines are the statements that perform the real work.

### Procedure Scope

Recall from Lesson 6, "About Variables," that scope refers to an item's sphere of action. Like variables, procedures can be Private to the form that they're defined in, meaning they're unavailable from other forms. They also can be made Public to any form in your application. To do this, you must put the procedure into a code module.

## Procedure Arguments

For public procedures in particular, you'll probably want to be able to hand off data to the procedure. Allowing a procedure to work directly with variables defined in other parts of your program usually isn't a good idea. Instead, you pass the procedure data through an argument list. This is just a list of variable names that the new procedure uses as temporary storage places for data being sent to it. Variable names for an argument list appear between the parentheses in the procedure's definition statement, as in the following example:

```
Sub MyNewProc (Name, Age)
```

If you don't specify otherwise, Visual Basic creates these new variables as Variants. Variant variables are, by definition, flexible, but indiscriminate use of Variants can cause problems down the road. It's better to make your variables and arguments a specific type if you can. To make arguments be specific data types, use the As keyword along with the variable type desired, as in:

```
Sub MyNewProc (Name As String, Age As Integer)
```

When the procedure is run, it uses the variables in the argument list to process data. This leads us to our last brief topic: how to make the procedure run once it's defined.

### Running a Procedure

To run a general procedure—a process referred to as *calling* the procedure—you need only put its name on a line, followed by values for the variables in the argument list. These values can be constants, or they can be variables themselves. To call the procedure MyNewProc for the name "Clint" and the age 34, you'd have this line:

```
MyNewProc "Clint",34
```

Alternatively, you can specify variable names:

```
MyNewProc FirstName,ClientAge
```

Note that these variable names are different from those in the procedure definition's argument list.

For the sake of readable code, however, you'll probably want to use the Call statement when running a procedure. Using Call to run the previous example, the statement becomes

```
Call MyNewProc FirstName,ClientAge
```

## Using Functions

There are times when you want a general procedure to respond back with a specific answer after you've sent it data to digest. Visual Basic procedures that do this—return a single answer—are called *functions*. Treat a function as you would any expression in an assignment statement. You can define your own functions, or you can use any of the many built-in functions Visual Basic provides. Figure 14.4 shows two function definitions in the code window.

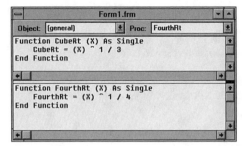

**Figure 14.4**
Two function definitions.

## Built-In Functions

Visual Basic includes dozens of predefined functions. These functions operate on both string and numeric data to produce text and mathematical results. The following is only a partial listing of the functions available. Note in particular the string functions; one of the great strengths of Visual Basic is the flexibility it gives you in handling strings.

| Function | Description |
| --- | --- |
| **Mathematical Functions** | |
| Abs | Show absolute value of number.<br>Abs(*numericexpression*) |
| Atn | Calculate arctangent of number; result in radians.<br>Atn(*numericexpression*) |
| Cos | Calculate cosine of specified angle, assumed to be in radians.<br>Cos(*numericexpression*) |
| Exp | Calculate natural antilogarithm of specified number.<br>Exp(*numericexpression*) |
| Int | Return the integer portion of the number supplied.<br>Int(*numericexpression*) |
| Log | Find natural logarithm of supplied number.<br>Log(*numericexpression*) |
| Sqr | Find square root of supplied number.<br>Sqr(*numericexpression*) |
| Tan | Calculate tangent of supplied angle, assumed to be in radians.<br>Tan(*numericexpression*) |

| Function | Description |
|----------|-------------|
| **String Functions** | |
| Asc | Return ASCII value of specified character.<br>Asc(*stringexpression*) |
| Chr$ | Return character string equivalent to specified ANSI code.<br>Chr$(*numericexpression*) |
| Date$ | Return character string equivalent to system date.<br>Date$ |
| Hex$ | Return string equivalent to hexadecimal value of supplied number.<br>Hex$(*numericexpression*) |
| InStr | Find first occurrence of one string within another, result returned as number.<br>InStr([*startposition*,]*StringToSearch*,*StringSearchedFor*) |
| Len | Calculate number of characters in a string expression.<br>Len(*stringexpression*) |
| Val | Converts string to number.<br>Val(stringexpression) |
| **System Functions** | |
| CurDir$ | Return character string equivalent to current directory.<br>CurDir$[(*drive*)] |
| Dir$ | Determine if the specified file or directory exists; finds a specific match if wildcard characters used. Returns the file or directory name if it exists; returns nothing if the file or directory doesn't exist.<br>Dir$(*pathname*) |
| FileLen | Return long integer equal to length of specified file, in bytes.<br>FileLen(*filename*) |
| RGB | Return long integer specifying an RGB color value, when supplied three integers in the range 0 to 255, representing levels of red, green, and blue respectively.<br>RGB(*red*, *green*, *blue*) |
| Shell | Run a program; like entering a command on DOS command line.<br>Shell(*stringexpression*)<br>Note: this function executes asynchronously; this means you can't assume the program you run with it will be finished before the remainder of the code in your Visual Basic program itself executes. |

II

Intermediate Topics

(continues)

| Function | Description |
|---|---|
| **Financial Functions** | |
| FV | Calculate future value of annuity.<br>FV(*rate*,<br>*NumberPeriods*,*Payment*,*PresentValue*,*DueFirstLast*)<br>Note: *DueFirstLast* is either 0 (end of period) or 1 (beginning of period). |
| NPV | Calculates net present value of an investment. Requires use of an array of cash flow values. At least one must be negative, representing a payment, and at least one must be positive, representing a receipt. Values in the array must be in the correct sequence.<br>NPV(*rate*,*cashflowarray*()) |
| Pmt | Find payment for an annuity.<br>Pmt(*Rate*,*NumberPeriods*,*PresentValue*,*FutureValue*,*DueWhen*?)<br>Note: *DueWhen*? must be 0 (end of period) or 1 (beginning). |
| Ucase$ | Convert supplied string expression to all uppercase.<br>UCase$(*stringexpression*) |

## Defining Your Own Functions

If there is some action you want to perform several times within your application, and you can't find a predefined function to do it, you easily can create your own. A function is simply a special type of procedure, declared with the Function keyword instead of Sub. The general form of a function definition is:

```
Function functionname (arguments) [As variabletype]
```

The arguments are names for variables through which the function acquires the data it is to work on. The optional As *variabletype* part of the definition lets you specify what kind of data the function is to return. For example, the following is a definition for a function to find the cube root of a number.

```
Function CubeRt (Cube) As Single
CubeRt=(Cube)^(1./3.)
End Function
```

**Note** Although we've spoken of functions as returning only a single value, you should know that a) a function can change the values of any parameter variables passed to it, and b) a function can change property values for forms and controls. Neither of these actions is necessarily considered good programming practice.

## Calling Functions

How do you invoke a function within your Visual Basic programs? You specify it by name, supplying constants or variable names in the place of the required arguments. For example, to call the CubeRt function previously defined, you'd use an assignment statement like:

```
Edge = CubeRt(Volume)
```

Because a function always returns a value, it acts like an expression within Visual Basic. Function calls appear on the right side of assignments statements, with the answer yielded by the function going into a variable on the left.

# Review

In this lesson, you learned the following:

☐ All program tasks in Visual Basic take place within procedures.

☐ Methods are predefined procedures for use with objects.

☐ Procedures are defined with the Sub keyword, and are invoked when called by name.

☐ Functions are procedures that return a single value as an answer.

☐ There are numerous predefined functions available in Visual Basic. You can find out about these in Visual Basic's online help.

## Quiz

Now you should be ready for the quiz.

## Lesson 15

# When Things Go Wrong: Handling Errors

## Overview

If only it were a perfect world, nothing would ever go wrong. It isn't, and stuff *does* go wrong. Even with your Visual Basic applications, mistakes are apt to be made. In this lesson, we'll show you some ways to deal with errors, no matter where and when they occur.

This lesson demonstrates, step-by-step, how to handle errors in a Visual Basic application program. Points covered include:

☐ Where problems might occur, and why

☐ How to look for and eliminate problems during program design

☐ Ways to deal with problems that might occur when a program is run

## Working Out Problems

There are few things as annoying as having your work interrupted by a computer bug. Computers (well, maybe not Pentium PCs) are supposed to be perfect, right? Actually, with notable exceptions, they are nearly perfect; it's computer software that harbors all the bugs, like the one shown in Figure 15.1.

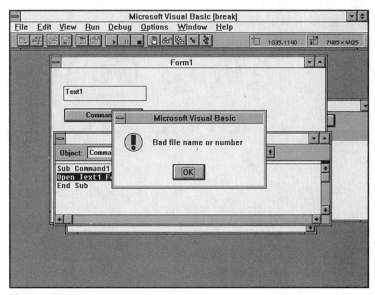

**Figure 15.1**
Oops! Visual Basic is telling us this program contains an error.

That there are relatively few errors in commercial software can be attributed to the (usually) careful and time-consuming way in which software developers chase down errors in their programs. Large companies like Microsoft usually spend months working out the bugs in their software, which is why major projects are sometimes so very late in coming to market. For a large project, such as a new version of Windows, there's plenty of room for errors to lurk.

Whether we're talking about a new operating system or a simple database access engine, a large corporation or a one-programmer shop, the process of eliminating errors is pretty much the same. A program is tested exhaustively to make sure that a) no egregious errors remain in the program code and b) the program behaves as expected in all cases that can be anticipated. This done, additional programming code is inserted so that the program can handle any remaining problems—usually assumed to be the fault of the user—gracefully. In this lesson we'll look at both processes.

## Problems during Development

During program development, the first kinds of errors you're likely to encounter are errors in compilation. These are a result of improperly entering Visual Basic programming code. Such errors are frequently referred to as *syntax errors*, as they result from improper Visual Basic language syntax. Misspelling a keyword, omitting a comma or a parenthesis, and failing to supply a needed parameter—all these are syntax errors.

In olden times, back when computer programs were prepared by punching cards, syntax errors were among the most annoying. Your humble author recalls only too well having an entire job rejected because a command was missing in a key statement. What made it worse was the job was submitted at 2:00 a.m. and the printout (revealing the error that kept the program from running) wasn't ready until 7:00.

Fortunately, you modern Visual Basic programmers don't have to put up with that sort of thing. Visual Basic has a syntax checking feature built into it. With this option selected, Visual Basic constantly monitors your code as you enter it, informing you immediately of any errors, as shown in Figure 15.2.

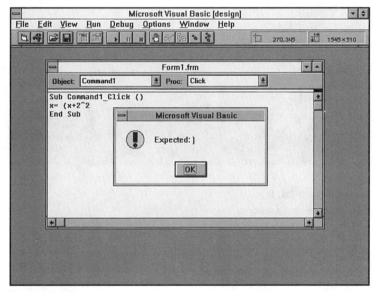

**Figure 15.2**
Syntax checking finds an error.

The other type of development error is trickier to spot. Such errors result from a program that doesn't quite do what it's supposed to in all cases. We call errors like this *logical errors*, because they represent a failure to accurately apply the rules of program logic on behalf of the programmer. It's up to you, the programmer, to find and eliminate such errors. You see, as far as the computer is concerned, there may never appear to be anything wrong; it executes your instructions as you entered them. It's just that the answer you get may not be correct.

Visual Basic does provide you with tools to help eliminate logic errors. Using the debug window, you can follow the execution of your program step-by-step, even to the point of always seeing the contents of crucial variables. Figure 15.3 shows the debug window.

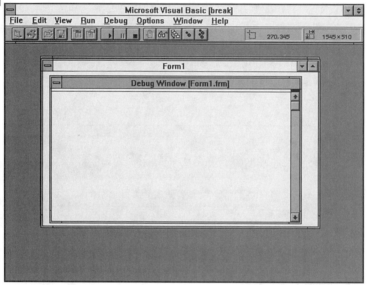

**Figure 15.3**
Debugging a suspect program.

## Problems at Run Time

Most runtime errors occur when your program attempts to do the impossible. This may be because conditions have changed in some way. Consider a program that needs to read from a floppy disk drive. If there is no disk in the drive, an error occurs. In another case, a program may attempt mathematical operations with bad data entered by the user.

Although, as a programmer, you can't prevent these sorts of problems, you can build code into your program that enables it to handle them. This procedure is called error trapping; it makes use of the error codes generated at run time when something goes wrong. You can write a specific procedure to be run for any error condition your program is likely to encounter.

Before moving on to such involved topics, however, we'll start out with the kinds of errors you can eliminate before a user ever sees your application.

# Debugging Your Program

The first thing to do is make sure your program doesn't contain syntax errors. Although you'll be informed of these fairly quickly when you try to compile and run your program, you can have such errors fingered as soon as you enter them if the Syntax Checking option is on. Note that syntax checking is "on" as a default. You set syntax checking by way of the Environment Options dialog box, accessed from the Visual Basic Options menu. Figure 15.4 shows the Environment Options dialog box.

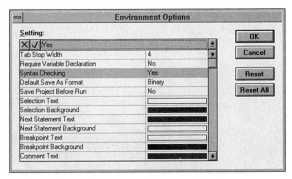

**Figure 15.4**
Setting Environment Options, including Syntax Checking.

Follow these steps to verify that syntax checking has been enabled, or to enable it if it's off:

1. With Visual Basic open, choose Environment... from the Options menu.

   The Environment Options dialog box appears.

2. Click to select Syntax Checking.

3. If Syntax checking is off (set to No), click the checkmark icon at the top of the dialog box.

The Syntax Checking setting changes to Yes.

4. Click OK to save the new setting and close the dialog box.

## About Break Mode

After you've entered all your program code and verified that its syntax is correct, the next step is to give your program a test drive. You do so by running it. If Visual Basic encounters an error while running, it breaks out of run mode and informs you of this fact. Such a message is shown in Figure 15.5.

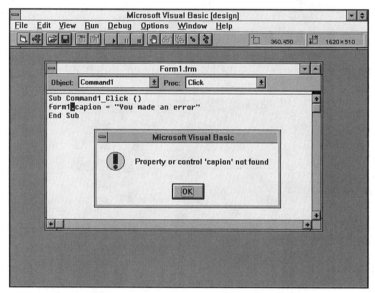

**Figure 15.5**
A program in break mode, with the accompanying message.

Note that the code window appears, with the offending statement highlighted. You can edit the problem immediately and continue running; click the Run button on the tool bar or choose Continue from the Run menu.

Sometimes a problem actually occurs farther up in a program, with a statement that appears to execute normally but actually creates problems for other statements later on. If you suspect some statement of causing such problems, you can manually instruct your program to stop execution at or around that statement. You do so by entering a breakpoint.

Follow this procedure to manually set a breakpoint for a given line of code:

1. With the Code window open, locate the line of code for which you want to set a breakpoint. Click to move the insert point into that line.

2. Choose Toggle Breakpoint from the Debug menu. You also may click the Breakpoint button on the tool bar, or press the F9 key.

3. Note that all breakpoints are cleared when you close a project or exit Visual Basic. You must reset them every time you load a project. You may clear all breakpoints immediately without quitting by choosing Clear All Breakpoints from the Debug menu.

## Watching the Value of Expressions

Visual Basic has a handy feature that lets you examine the contents of any variables or expressions in the current procedure, to make certain they're correct. You do so using the Instant Watch command. You merely select the code whose contents you want to know, and choose Instant Watch. Figure 15.6 shows what happens when you do this.

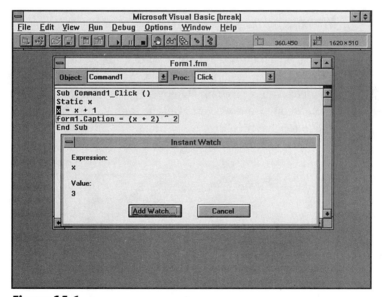

**Figure 15.6**
The Instant Watch dialog.

Take these steps to examine an expression's contents while in Break mode:

1. In break mode, with the Code window open, find and select the expression you want to evaluate.

2. Choose Instant Watch from the Debug menu. You also may click the Instant Watch button on the tool bar, or press Shift+F9.

   A dialog box appears, showing the selected expression and its value. An example of this dialog box is shown in Figure 15.6.

3. Note that you may set a Watch expression immediately for anything you've selected in Instant Watch. Click the Add Watch button on the dialog box to do so.

   A dialog box like that shown in Figure 15.7 appears.

4. You must set the context (where to watch the expression) and how to watch (such as whether to break program execution when the expression changes). Make changes to watch expressions using the Edit Watch command in the Debug menu.

## More about the Debugger

The Visual Basic Debug Window, which always appears when you enter a manual breakpoint, is a useful tool in a couple of ways. It displays the value of all watch expressions. You then can examine how their contents change as you execute a program step-by-step, for example. In the Immediate pane of the Debug window, you can type sample lines of code and check to see what happens when they're executed. You also can view the contents of variables for which no watch expression is set. Figure 15.7 shows an example.

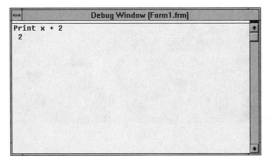

**Figure 15.7**
Using the Immediate pane on the Debug window.

The following steps show how to step through a program:

1. Set watch expressions as desired.

2. Set breakpoints as needed.

3. Step through the program. Choose Single Step from the Debug menu. You also may click the Single Step icon on the tool bar, or press the F8 button.

Take these steps to immediately examine the results of a statement or expression:

1. In Break mode, move the insertion point to the Immediate Pane of the Debug window.

2. To evaluate the effects of a statement, simply type it into the Immediate Pane.

   Visual Basic switches to Run mode just long enough to execute the statement, which can be a procedure call.

3. To determine the value of a variable for which no watch expression has been set, use the `Print` method. Enter **Print**, followed by the name of the variable. You may use a question mark in the place of the keyword `Print`. This method also will reveal the settings of object properties.

## Debugging Hints

Unfortunately, it isn't possible to outline a general procedure that will show you exactly how to debug any program. That's because all programs are different, working with different data under varying conditions. The best we can do at this point is offer some general advice for how to go about debugging a program.

Keep these ideas in mind as you debug your application:

☐ The best way to eliminate bugs is to try assiduously to avoid them in the first place. Be careful with naming variables, and keep good track of what each procedure is supposed to do, and the kind of data it expects.

**II**

Intermediate Topics

☐ Set watch expressions for all your most important variables. Recall that you can set these expressions to cause a break in the program whenever the expression's contents change.

☐ Test program execution with every conceivable combination of data.

☐ Try doing things the user isn't supposed to do when your program is running. Can it handle abuse?

☐ Try stepping through your program to make sure it behaves the way you expect.

# Catching Errors during Execution

You might think that a totally debugged program would be bullet-proof, but you'd be wrong if you did. Recall one of Murphy's corollaries: "You can't make anything fool-proof, because fools are far too ingenious." Without disparaging the intelligence and wisdom of your program users further, let's just say that people make mistakes: they key in the wrong data, they leave disk drive doors open, they forget to turn on printers, they supply names of files that have been deleted, and so on. While you can't prevent such errors, you can construct your program so that it reacts graciously, rather than crashing and burning, when the user makes a mistake.

## Dealing with Typical Execution Problems

Ways in which you deal with runtime errors divide, of course, into two categories. You can write code that tries to screen out potential data entry errors by the user—code that rejects character keys when the user is supposed to type numbers, for example. For errors that can't be anticipated in this way, you can devise a special routine to run whenever an error is encountered.

### Validating User Input

Typically, the only place a user might input bad data is in some form of text box. An error will occur if your program expects number data and the user enters characters. A way to deal with this is to have an event procedure for the text box associated with the Keypress event. The procedure evaluates each keystroke the user enters; if it's out of range, the procedure cancels the keystroke and sounds a beep. Figure 15.8 shows such a procedure in the Code window.

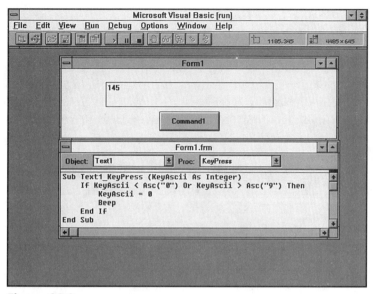

**Figure 15.8**
A procedure that cancels keystrokes.

In other instances, a user may enter data that is of the correct type, but doesn't make sense otherwise. Entering "0" as the amount of a payment on an installment loan is an example. A zero in the wrong place might cause an attempt to divide by zero, which is impossible. You can trap such an error by testing the value of variables or expressions to make sure they aren't zero. This can be done either at input time, or during execution. Figure 15.9 shows a simple error-trapping routine.

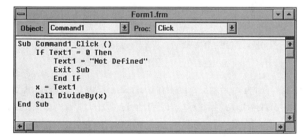

**Figure 15.9**
A procedure to trap out-of-range data.

### Runtime Error Handling

To work around errors in execution that might occur during run time, and which cannot be trapped by testing input, you need to write special code to handle them. Whenever such an error occurs, Visual Basic generates an error number. By evaluating this error number in an error-handling procedure you write, you can have the program determine what course of action to take. Figure 15.10 shows such an error-handling routine in the Code window.

```
┌─────────────────────────────────────────────────┐
│ ─              Form1.frm                    ▼ ▲   │
│ Object: Command1    ± Proc: Click           ±     │
├─────────────────────────────────────────────────┤
│ Sub Command1_Click ()                          ▲  │
│ On Error GoTo ErrorHandler                        │
│ FileNumber = FreeFile                             │
│ Drive = C:                                        │
│ Open Drive & Text1.Text For Input As FileNumber   │
│ Exit Sub                                          │
│                                                   │
│ ErrorHandler:                                     │
│ MsgBox "Cannot find the file you requested", 64, "Error" │
│ Exit Sub                                          │
│ End Sub                                        ▼  │
│ ◄ └───────────────────────────────────────┘ ►    │
└─────────────────────────────────────────────────┘
```

**Figure 15.10**
Trapping and dealing with errors at run time.

The foundation of any procedure to trap runtime errors and deal with them is the On Error statement. On Error tells the program to transfer execution to a specified location if an error occurs. The Err keyword represents a variable containing the error code generated during the error. Your error-handling routine can test the contents of Err and then determine what to do based on the results of the test. The On Error statement takes the form:

```
On Error GoTo linelabel
```

We have not encountered anything like *linelabel* to this point. A line label is used to refer to a specific section of code within the procedure; the label occurs on a line by itself, followed by a colon.

Note that an error-trapping routine enabled by `On Error` is only active within the procedure that created it; when that procedure is exited, Error Trapping is disabled. Thus, you must have an error-trapping routine for each procedure apt to encounter runtime errors. To exit an error-trapping routine without exiting the procedure it's in, include the statement `Resume` as the last line in the routine; this transfers execution back to the statement that caused the error. To leave the procedure entirely, include `Exit Sub` as the last line in the error-trapping routine.

## Handling "Cancel" in the Common Dialog Control

Before we close, there's a special case error we need to talk about. You may recall back in Lesson 11, "About Dialog Boxes," we stated that when the user clicks Cancel on a common dialog box, an error is actually generated. You must have an appropriate error-handling routine ready for this error; otherwise, your program won't cancel out of the dialog box correctly. In such a case, your program might even behave as if the OK button had been clicked instead.

To avoid this, the `CancelError` property for the common dialog control is set to True. Figure 15.11 shows one way to handle the error generated by clicking Cancel when `CancelError` is enabled.

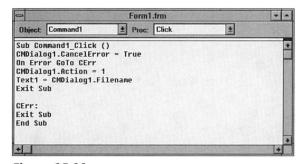

```
Form1.frm
Object: Command1    Proc: Click

Sub Command1_Click ()
CMDialog1.CancelError = True
On Error GoTo CErr
CMDialog1.Action = 1
Text1 = CMDialog1.Filename
Exit Sub

CErr:
Exit Sub
End Sub
```

**Figure 15.11**
Handling common dialog Cancel.

# Review

In this lesson, you learned the following:

☐ Errors occur both when a program is being developed and when the user runs it. The former are syntax or logical errors; the latter are referred to as runtime errors.

☐ Using syntax checking, an option with the Environment dialog box, you can have Visual Basic evaluate statements for syntax errors as they're entered.

☐ You can trap logical errors within Break mode. Adding Watch expressions lets you see the contents of critical variables and expressions. The Immediate pane of the Debug window, which appears when a manual breakpoint is encountered, can be used to test execution of

**II**

Intermediate Topics

specific statements, and to view the contents of variables with the `Print` method.

☐ One way to trap errors at run time is to screen user input to make sure data entered is of the correct type. Such a routine cancels a keystroke if it doesn't correspond to the correct data type. Routines also can be constructed to check for invalid values, such as zero in the case of division.

☐ Another way to trap runtime errors is to use the `On Error GoTo` statement to construct an error-handling routine. `On Error` tells the program what place to transfer execution to if an error condition occurs. It's up to the programmer to write a routine that deals with the exact error encountered, whose error number will be found in the *Err* variable.

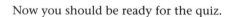

Now you should be ready for the quiz.

# Part III
## Advanced Topics

# More on Objects: Arrays and Instances

## Overview

One critical goal of application programming is to make applications as flexible as possible, while preserving scarce system resources. An area of concern in this regard is a program's storage requirements for variables. For example, you might write a program that allows the user to open a large number of document windows. Each of these, however, can take up a significant amount of computer memory. If you define a separate form for each possible window at design time, you risk tying up memory. What's more, your user will actually be limited; windows can only be opened for as many forms as you designed.

A better way to handle such situations is to include programming code that creates storage—whether for forms, controls, or even variables—at run time. Such storage can be allocated and released as needed, offering flexibility while saving memory. In this lesson, we'll examine ways to do this.

This lesson looks at dynamic allocation of certain system resources. We'll examine:

- ☐ How to create arrays of controls

- ☐ Ways to let variable arrays grow or shrink to fit user needs

- ☐ Methods for cloning new objects, such as forms, while a program is running

# Many Objects from One Definition

If you've worked very much with current word processing software, you should be familiar with document templates. In brief, a *template* is a generic document with specific style settings. You use templates to create new documents with these same settings. Templates save a lot of work, and they also help standardize the format for things such as memos and fax cover sheets.

It turns out that Visual Basic has several ways to create new resources from existing templates. These capabilities also can save a lot of work, in addition to giving your programs the ability to handle a wider range of conditions. Though these Visual Basic "templates" work with different things—arrays and objects—they all offer the ability to use a single, prototype entity as a basis for creating a great many more useful tools.

## Control Arrays

One of the simplest ways to clone several objects from one definition is to create control arrays. Such a group of controls is very similar to an array variable. Each control in an array can be exactly the same as all others; the only difference is its index.

Like an array variable, a control array has an index property. The value of this property specifies which control is actually being referred to. Figure 16.1 shows a control array on a form, with the Properties window open to show the settings for the array.

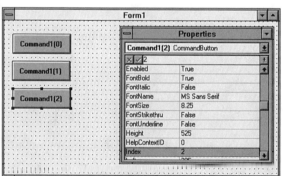

**Figure 16.1**
A control array and its properties.

Note that you create control arrays at design time.

## Resources at Run Time

Additional Visual Basic flexibility is available through allocation of resources at run time. You can set the size of an array variable at run time. You also can have an entirely new object, such as a form, created at run time as well.

### Dynamically Resizing Arrays

You can't always anticipate how much storage space you'll need for a program at design time. Probably the worst thing that might happen is to design an array that's too small. Users don't like it when there isn't enough space to store all their data. Creating a very large array, on the other hand, wastes computer memory. Users don't like it when programs run out of memory, either.

What to do? Visual Basic lets you create variable arrays whose size is set at run time. You can have the program query the user as to how many items of data they want to enter, for example, and then have the program create an array to match the data. A truly clever programmer could think of ways to create and use dynamic arrays that wouldn't even need that much input from the user. Figure 16.2 shows the code needed to create a dynamic-variable array.

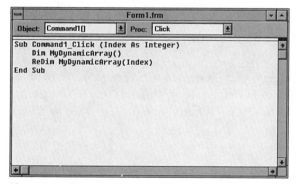

**Figure 16.2**
Code for a dynamically sized array.

III

Advanced Topics

### Object Variables and Instances

Another thing program users like is the ability to open as many documents within an application as they've got computer memory to support. You can see already that it is impractical to include a separate form in your Visual Basic application for every window a user might want open. Instead, you can let Visual Basic create forms (and other objects) at will using object variables. At design time, you include code in your program that sets an object variable equal to a new incarnation of a previously defined object. Figure 16.3 shows the code used to create a new form out of an existing one, also shown.

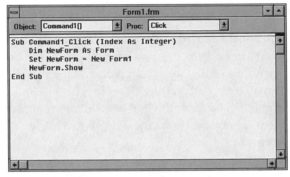

```
Sub Command1_Click (Index As Integer)
    Dim NewForm As Form
    Set NewForm = New Form1
    NewForm.Show
End Sub
```

**Figure 16.3**
Creating a new instance of a predefined object, in this case, a form.

Using all (or part) of these nifty tricks can prepare your program to handle a wide range of eventualities, without having to tie up a lot of system resources. For specifics on how to use these goodies, we'll start with control arrays.

## About Control Arrays

Why use control arrays? They're handy when you need a single general procedure with variations. You can let each of the variations correspond to one member of the array. For example, you might have a menuing system in which each button on a form corresponds to a menu choice. Suppose the only difference is what text is displayed in a help pane on the form. In this case, the index number of the button clicked would be the only information needed to determine what text to display. The rest of the procedure could be entirely general and used no matter what button the user clicked.

Creating a control array is quite easy, after you've created a single prototype control to serve as the basis for the remainder of the array. You only need to set the index property for each array element and then write code for the array as a whole. We'll look at each step in turn.

### Defining a Control Array

The Index property is the key to creating control arrays. Normally, the Index property of any control is blank. Setting the Index property to any value at all automatically creates an array. As with variable arrays, the first element in a control array usually has an index value of 0. So in brief, the way to create a control array is to define a control, copy it, paste in new copies on the form for each element in the array beyond the first, and set the indexes.

Use these steps to create a control array at design time:

1. Select and drag out a control on the appropriate form. Press F4 to access the Properties window.

2. Set properties for the control, including its name. Close the Properties window.

3. Select the control, and copy it to the Clipboard using the Edit menu's Copy command.

4. Paste a new copy of the control onto the form, using the Edit menu's Paste command.

   A dialog box appears, like that shown in Figure 16.4, asking if you want to create a control array. Click Yes.

**Figure 16.4**
Confirming creation of a control array.

5. Continue to paste controls until the desired number is reached. Drag individual controls to arrange them on the form.

6. Choosing each control in turn, access the Properties window and set the control's Index property to the desired number. Each control must have a unique index number.

Note that earlier we said that all controls in an array can be exactly the same; however, they don't have to be. Although all members of an array must be of the same control type (all command buttons, for example) and must have the same name, which is the name of the array, all their other property settings can be different. They don't all have to visible, for example. With this in mind, you can create an array of controls, a variable number of which is available to the user at any time, depending on your program's needs.

## Control Array Procedures

Once created, elements in a control array are referred to just as you refer to elements in an array variable, using the array name and an index value. Thus, Command1(1) refers to the member of the Command1 array with index value 1; Command1() refers to the entire array.

Because each element in a control array shares a common name, you can define only one procedure for each event for the array as a whole; you can't have individual click procedures, for example, for each element in the array. Rather than a limitation, however, this is actually one of the most useful features of a control array. A single general procedure handles clicks (or other events) for every member of the array. Figure 16.5 shows a Command_Click procedure for a control array.

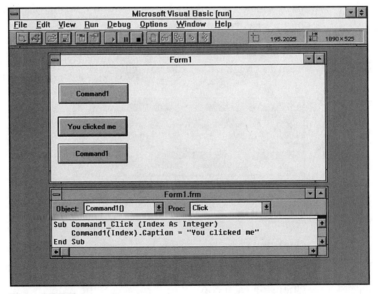

**Figure 16.5**
A control array event procedure.

Use these steps to define a procedure for a control array:

1. Double-click any member of the array to open the code window. Choose which event to define from the drop-down list at the top of the window.

   The code window generally opens ready to define the Click procedure, so you can omit choosing the event if you want to define Click.

2. Type Visual Basic statements to define the procedure.

3. To determine which member of the array was invoked, examine the Index variable, which is provided as an argument to the procedure. Index contains an integer corresponding to the index number of the control chosen by the user.

A handy structure to use when programming control arrays is the Select Case statement. You can write a separate case corresponding to each member of the control array. Figure 16.6 shows an example of a control array procedure written using Select Case.

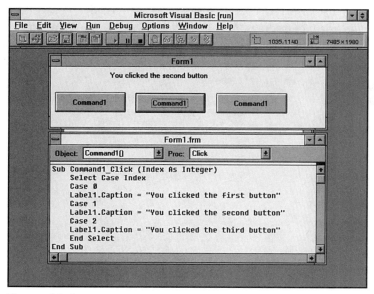

**Figure 16.6**
A control array event procedure using Select Case.

**Note** You can add or remove elements in a control array at run time. You do this using the Load and Unload statements. The general form of such a statement is

Load *ControlArrayName*(*IndexNumber*)

Property settings are copied from the lowest-numbered element in the existing control array. You may, of course, include statements to change these settings after the control is created. You will probably need to specify position properties for the new element.

# Sizing Arrays at Run Time

Control arrays aren't the only thing you can add to or take away from at run time. It's also quite useful to be able to change the size of an array variable. This lets the array grow or shrink to meet circumstances. Such arrays are called dynamic arrays. You declare them at design time; their exact size is determined within program code when your program is run.

### Declaring a Dynamic Array

The first thing to do is determine what scope you want the array to have. Use the Global keyword within a code module to make the array available to all procedures in your program. Use Dim within a procedure to make the array local to that procedure only. Beyond that, you need only to omit the index arguments to create a dynamic array. Figure 16.7 shows declarations for three dynamic arrays.

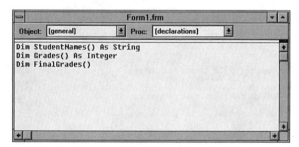

**Figure 16.7**
Creating three dynamic arrays.

The following demonstrates how to create a dynamic array:

1. Open the code window within the module for which you're creating the array.

2. For a local array, type **Dim** followed by the array name, followed by empty parentheses.

## Allocating a Dynamic Array at Run Time

Before you can actually use a dynamic array, you must tell Visual Basic to allocate storage for it. You do so within a procedure using the ReDim statement. This statement tells Visual Basic to redimension the array with the parameters you supply.

A ReDim statement follows the form:

```
ReDim DynamicArrayName(ArgumentExpressionList)
```

The expression list contains one expression for each dimension in the array. Note that you can use variables in the expression list; in this way, the exact size of the array may be determined and set at run time based on the value of other variables in your program. For example, to allocate a two-dimensional array called Grades, which maintains a variable number of test grades for a variable-sized class, you can include a ReDim statement in your program like:

```
ReDim Grades(NumberStudents,NumberExams)
```

The exact size of the array at run time depends on the values contained in the two variables NumberStudents and NumberExams.

## Preserving Array Contents

There's an important thing you need to know about the ReDim statement: each time it's run, the previous contents of the array being redimensioned are wiped out. In many cases, this doesn't matter. However, if you're trying to add new elements to an existing array that happens to be full, wiping out the array with ReDim can be disastrous.

To avoid wiping out an array when using ReDim, use the Preserve keyword in the ReDim statement. Note that you may only use this form of ReDim when you are adding to the last dimension in the array. Doing anything else results in an error. The function UBound, which takes the array name and index number as arguments, gives the current limit of the named dimension. Thus, a statement of the form

```
ReDim Preserve DynamicArrayName(UBound(DynamicArrayName,1) + 1)
```

adds one element to the named one-dimensional array.

# Creating Objects at Run Time

You can add elements to an array at run time, so how about adding other things? You can. To do this, you must first understand something about object variables, which are entities Visual Basic uses to manipulate objects (forms and controls) at run time.

## About Object Variables

An object variable is used to "contain" an object, just as regular variables contain data. Object variables come in specific types, just as regular variables do. An object variable's type variable is set when you create it, using any of the statements Dim, Static, or Global, depending on what scope you want the variable to have. Figure 16.8 shows declarations for two object variables.

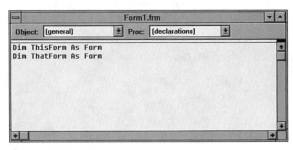

**Figure 16.8**
Creating object variables.

The general form for declaring a local object variable is

    Dim *ObjectVariableName* As [New] *ObjectType*

The ObjectType parameter can be any type of object supported by Visual Basic: a form, a command button, and so on. To declare an object variable capable of referring to a form, you'd use something like:

    Dim AnyForm As Form

## Creating Object Instances

You use the New keyword when you want to refer to a new instance of a previously defined form. (You can't create a new, specific instance of a control.) The form referred to must exist in your project. Supposing you have a form named `DocumentForm`, and you want to create a new instance of that form. The statement

```
Dim NewForm As New DocumentForm
```

creates an object variable named `NewForm` that refers to a new instance of `DocumentForm`.

You also can create new instances of a form using the Set keyword and an existing form-type object variable. This is a more general way of creating new form instances and a safer one at that. Creating a new instance of a specific form by dimensioning a variable of that specific type could result in a type-mismatch error later on. The following two lines of code create a generic form variable named NewForm and set it equal to a new instance of an existing form named DocumentForm:

```
Dim NewForm as Form
Set NewForm = New DocumentForm
```

Thereafter, you can use the object variable in the place of the form name in any statement, such as those assigning property values to a form. Changing the caption on a newly created instance of a form is as easy having the line:

```
NewForm.Caption = "This is a new form"
```

## Working with Multiple Form Instances

Each instance of a form has its own variables, properties, and procedures, although these are identical to (if separate from) the original form's qualities. Usually, there's no need to distinguish between instances.

Sometimes, though, when you're working with multiple instances of a form, it's handy for your programming code to be able to determine which instance is which. Your code can always determine which instance of a form is active using the Me keyword. This keyword always refers to the form in which the current procedure is actually running. For example, to unload the currently running form, all you need to supply to the Unload method is the keyword Me.

You also can set a form variable equal to a current form instance using the Me keyword. Such a statement has the form:

```
Set FormVariableName = Me
```

If you need to keep track of which form instance was active using a global form variable, you can include such code in the `Form_GotFocus` event procedure for the original form from which the instances were cloned.

# Review

In this lesson, you learned the following:

☐ Using the control index property, you can create arrays of controls. A control array is a collection of controls of the same type. Although the controls may have different properties (other than their name, which is the name of the entire array), they share all procedures. The index number of a particular array member is passed to the appropriate event procedure when an event occurs to that particular control array member.

☐ Using the ReDim statement, you can create arrays whose exact size is set at run time. These dynamic arrays are first created in the variable's declaration stage, using an empty set of parentheses after the array name.

☐ Using object variables, it's possible to create new instances of a pre-defined form at run time. The Set statement is used to attach a particular generic object variable to a specific object instance, which is created with the New keyword.

Now you should be ready for the quiz.

## Lesson 17

# Storing, Retrieving, and Printing Data

## Overview

In our ongoing examination of things users like, how could we leave out saving and recalling data? To be really useful, after all, most applications need to be able to put data into long-term storage, so that it can be worked with at a later time, with the computer safely powered off between sessions. It's also quite helpful to be able to put data into an even more nearly permanent form: on paper. Folks still seem to find the printed page useful as a storage and retrieval medium. In this lesson, we'll take a glance at the tools Visual Basic provides for working with files, and for printing.

This lesson looks at working with the Windows file system. Topics covered include:

- ☐ Available controls for working with the file system
- ☐ Ways to access data stored in files
- ☐ How to create new files and read data from existing ones
- ☐ How to print using the `Printer` object and the `Print` method, as well as using the `PrintForm` method

## Moving Data between an Application and Windows

To store or print data, you need to be able to move it between your Visual Basic application and the Microsoft Windows file system. Your application also must be able to present the file system to the user in a way that makes sense and is consistent with the way other applications present the same information. Naturally, Visual Basic provides tools and procedures to make all these things relatively easy to program.

## File System Controls

Visual Basic has three file system-related controls. These controls let you create directory list boxes, drive list boxes, and file list boxes. A combination of these three boxes enables the user to navigate through the file system, either to look for a particular file by name, or to find an appropriate directory location in which to store a new file. Figure 17.1 shows all three controls together on a form.

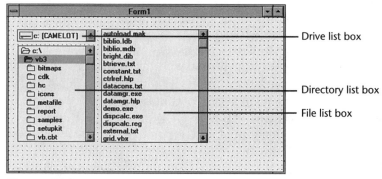

**Figure 17.1**
Drive, directory, and file list boxes on a form.

It's worth noting that all three boxes appear together on the common dialog control, which you learned about in Lesson 11, "About Dialog Boxes."

## Storing and Retrieving Data

While the file system controls enable the program user to navigate in the directory structure, additional resources are required to actually move data to and from that structure. You use the Open statement to create a new file or to open an existing one for data access and possible modification. Figure 17.2 shows an example of a procedure to open a file specified by the user.

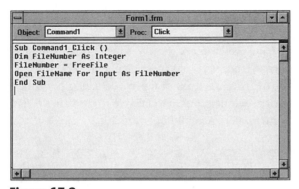

**Figure 17.2**
Opening a file to read text data from it.

## Printing

You might think that getting your application to print would be the hardest thing of all, but actually it's quite simple. Visual Basic has a predefined `Printer` object, which provides a bridge between your program and Microsoft Windows printing. You can send individual data items directly to the `Printer` object, and then have the entire collection printed when appropriate. Alternatively, you can define a print form and have the entire form printed. Figure 17.3 shows both methods.

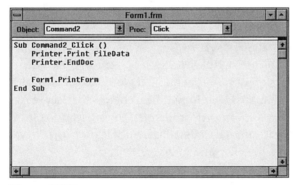

**Figure 17.3**
Ways to print from within a Visual Basic program.

All roads in this chapter seem to lead to the file system and controls to manipulate it, so that's where we'll start.

III

**Advanced Topics**

# Accessing the File System

Those who have ever had occasion to save or open a file have experienced the joys of the Windows file system. Generally, you work with this system through the use of some form of Open File dialog box, like that shown in Figure 17.4. The whole point is to be able to provide a file name to some procedure intended to actually open the file.

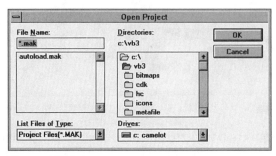

**Figure 17.4**
The Open Project dialog box, used to look for a particular project file.

While you could use the Common Dialog control to create a dialog box like that shown in Figure 17.4, you also can use the File System controls to accomplish the same thing. Doing so lets you customize an Open dialog box to meet the needs of your own application.

## File System Controls

You can think of the three File System controls from Visual Basic as three special types of list boxes. Recall that we looked at using list boxes in Lesson 13, "Additional User Input." The choices the user makes at run time are stored in the Drive or Path property of the relevant file system control. Your program code must take advantage of these properties to get the three controls to work together smoothly.

### Drive List Box

The drive list box shows all current available drives. When the user clicks a choice on this list box, the Drive property of the list box is updated to contain the user's choice. Using a ChDrive statement in a subsequent procedure, with the Drive property's contents as an argument, will then change the current drive to the one the user selected. Figure 17.5 shows programming code associated with a drive list box.

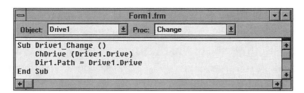

**Figure 17.5**
Defining a drive list box.

### Directory List Box

The directory list box can be set to use the contents of the drive list box's Drive property. The directory list box will then show all directories on the current drive. Figure 17.6 shows code written to enable a directory list box.

**Figure 17.6**
Defining a directory list box.

One useful property of the directory list box is its ListIndex property. The contents of this property identify which item the user selected. ListIndex = -1 is assigned to the current directory, ListIndex = 0 is the item on the list immediately below it, ListIndex = -2 is the item immediately above it, and so on.

When the user single-clicks an item in the directory list box, that item is highlighted. When the user double-clicks an item, its value is stored in the Path property of the directory list box, and the item gets a ListIndex property of -1. You then can use a ChDir statement in your code, using the Path property as an argument, to change the directory to the one the user selected.

### File List Box

The file list box shows all files in the directory specified by its Path property. Names of all the files are stored in the list box's List property, which is an array. You can set the Path property equal to the value of the Path property belonging to the directory list box. The ultimate choice the user makes is stored in the FileName property, which is only available at run time. Thus, subsequent code in your application should use the Path property of the file list along with the value of the FileName property to determine what file was selected by the user. Figure 17.7 shows code to enable a file list box.

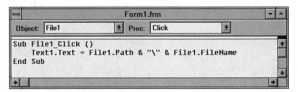

**Figure 17.7**
Defining a file list box.

## Working with Files

After you retrieve a file name, what next? You need to actually find the file's data and move it into (or out of) your application to work with or save it. The first thing you need to know about this process is the different ways in which you can access a file's data.

### Types of File Access

How you get to a file's data depends on the type of file you'll be working with. There are three kinds of file access:

| Access Method | Purpose |
| --- | --- |
| Random | Looks at database files, or other files in which the data is stored as individual records. Each record has an identical length, and consists of one or more fields, each holding some type of data |
| Sequential | Examines plain text or other ASCII files. This access type is most suited for working in text and line editors |
| Binary | The most general access form. No assumptions are made about the kind of data stored; it's up to your program to interpret data. This form of access is difficult to program, but is much used for applications that produce documents with their own file formats, such as word processors and graphics programs |

Because random and binary access are tricky to learn, we'll restrict examples in the remainder of this chapter to using sequential access. Whatever access form you use, however, the steps to working with file data are roughly the same:

1. Use the `Open` statement to access the file for `Input` purposes.

2. Read data from the file into program variables.

3. Release the file using the `Close` statement.

4. Perform modifications to the file data as desired.

5. Reopen the file for `Output`.

6. Write data from program variables back to the file.

7. Close the file again.

Now we'll look at some examples of reading and writing file data.

### Retrieving File Data

You use the `Open` statement with the `Input` keyword to set a file so that data may be read from it. This statement takes the form:

```
Open FileName For Input As FileNumber
```

Note the use of the *FileNumber* parameter. After a file is opened, it's always referred to using this file number. You can use the `FreeFile` function to obtain a valid file number. The following examples presume that `CurrentFile` is a string variable containing a file name, and that *FileNumber* is an integer variable. This code will open the file whose name is stored in `CurrentFile`:

```
FileNumber=FreeFile
Open CurrentFile For Input as FileNumber
```

After a file has been opened, you use various versions of the `Input` statement to copy data from the file into variables within your program. The two forms of this statement read either single lines from the file, or the entire file at once.

Forms of the file Input statement include:

| Statement | Purpose |
| --- | --- |
| `Line Input #` | Reads a line from a file into a specified variable. Each time this statement is executed, the number of the current line within the file is increased by 1.<br>`Line Input #FileNumber, VariableName` |

(continues)

| Statement | Purpose |
|-----------|---------|
| Input$ | Copies specified number of characters of file. Use this form of the Input statement in an assignment statement.<br>Input$ (*NumberCharacters, FileNum*) |
| Input # | Reads list of values from file.<br>Input #*FileNumber, VariableList* |

Once you've gotten data from a file into your application, you should use the Close statement to release the file. This statement takes the form Close *FileNumber*.

### Storing File Data

After your program has finished manipulating text data, it's time to reopen the original file and copy the changed data backed to it. This is also done using the Open statement; data is copied back using the Print # statement.

To open a file so that data may be written back to it, use a statement of the form:

```
Open FileName for Output As FileNumber
```

**Note**  Be aware that you can use this statement to create a file that didn't previously exist. (If you try to open a nonexistent file for Input, you'll generate an error.) If the file doesn't exist, the file system creates it and gives it the specified name.

Once the file is open, use the Print # statement to copy data from the specified variable back to the file. Note that this will completely replace the previous file contents, so be careful. This statement takes the form:

```
Print #FileNumber, VariableName
```

**Caution**  Be careful using the Print # statement. Again, it completely replaces the file's previous contents. This means indiscriminant use of this statement can destroy data. To prevent this, use the Dir$ function in your program to determine whether the file already exists. Then, present an alert box that allows the user to cancel the operation and choose another name. The following lines of code do just that.

```
If Dir$(FileName) <> ""      ' If Dir$ doesn't return a null value,
                             ' the file exists
    Response = MsgBox("Overwrite File?",
            305, "File already exists"
    Select Case Response
```

```
            Case 1
                    Exit Select     ' Do nothing if user clicks OK
            Case 2
                    Exit Sub        ' Exit the sub if user clicks Cancel
        End Select
End If
```

If you want to add to, rather than replace, a file's contents, open it using the `Append` keyword rather than `Output`, as in:

```
Open FileName for Append as FileNumber
```

Remember to include a statement to `Close` the file after data has been copied to it.

# Printing

Moving data to that other storage medium—paper—isn't so difficult as copying it to disk. In some ways, you can think of Visual Basic as having an already opened file to which you may copy data you want to print using the current system printer. This file is called the `Printer` object.

## About the Printer Object

The `Printer` object has the same characteristics as the current system printer. These characteristics include the page size and orientation and the current font selection. The `Printer` object also has `CurrentX` and `CurrentY` properties, which specify the page location at which objects will be printed. Note that you may use the runtime graphics commands—such as `Line` and `Circle`—to draw graphics directly to the `Printer` object for output.

To put something onto the `Printer` object for later printing, you use the `Print` method. Following a `Print` method statement by the name of a variable prints the contents of that variable onto the `Printer` object at the current X and Y position. The statement follows the form:

```
Printer.Print VariableName
```

To send the contents of the `Printer` object to the system printer, use the `EndDoc` method. Thus, the statement:

```
Printer.EndDoc
```

sends whatever happens to have been copied onto the `Printer` object to the system printer. Figure 17.8 shows code that will copy the contents of a text box to the `Printer` object and then print it when the user chooses Print from the application's File menu.

III
Advanced Topics

**Figure 17.8**
Simple code for printing text.

## Printing a Form

There's a down and dirty printing method that bypasses the Printer object altogether. The PrintForm method immediately sends a bit-by-bit copy of the specified form (or the current form if none is specified) to the system printer. Because a bitmapped image is being sent, this method does not achieve results as good as the Printer object when you're sending output to a laser printer. The inferior print quality will be most obvious in printing text. Figure 17.9 shows code that prints the current form.

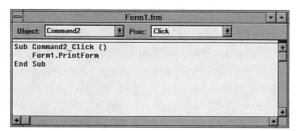

**Figure 17.9**
Using the PrintForm method.

# Review

In this lesson, we saw that:

☐ You can use the drive, directory, and file list box controls to enable the user to navigate in the file system.

☐ File data can be accessed randomly, for looking at database records; sequentially, for examining text data; and in binary form, for looking at formatted files.

□ You use various forms of the Open statement to prepare a file to be read from or written to.

□ The Printer object is used to send data to the system printer. You use the Print method to copy data to the Printer object, and the EndDoc method to send that data over to the system printer. The PrintForm method offers a shortcut for printing an entire form that bypasses the Printer object.

Now you should be ready for the quiz.

## Lesson 18

# Communicating with Other Programs

## Overview

Computing is just filled with buzzwords, isn't it? RAM, ROM, object-oriented programming—the list goes on and on. In the last few years, perhaps no single term on the buzzword list has attracted quite as much attention as *inter-application communications*. The interest is justified. Enabling computer applications to talk to each other makes it much easier to share data and construct complex documents. In this lesson, we'll introduce you to a couple of ways that Visual Basic lets you construct applications that can communicate with other Windows programs.

This lesson looks at working with other applications using the database and OLE controls. Topics covered include:

☐ What inter-application communications are all about

☐ How to use the Database control to link to existing database documents

☐ About Object Linking and Embedding (OLE), and how to use the OLE container control to link to or embed objects from other Windows applications that support the OLE standard

III

Advanced Topics

# Accessing Data from Other Applications

Windows applications can be fairly specialized; the work one needs to do these days may not be. Think of it: A person might need to create a report with charts, graphics, and formatted text. To do this, our intrepid worker uses a spreadsheet program to make the charts, a graphics program to make the illustrations, and a word processor to write the text. After that, the final document has to be assembled. Clearly, whatever program is used to assemble the ultimate report has to at least be aware of the ways that the other programs store their data.

Now add a complication. Suppose this report is being prepared by an entire team of workers, with each component (charts, graphics, and so on) being created by someone different. Each of these components is likely to go through several revisions as its author refines and adds to it. So what happens to the final document when someone makes a last minute change to one of the component parts? Unless someone else takes the trouble to re-open that document and incorporate the changes into it, the final report may not be accurate. The problem gets truly daunting if each part depends on data contained in the others. Add a tight deadline, which is *always* the case, and you have a recipe for a real mess.

It would be really nice—and this is why inter-application communications is so hot—if, rather than copying data by hand from other applications, you could create a "link" to that data so that any changes made to it are automatically incorporated into the final product. An architect who needed to produce a door schedule, showing the type and number of doors in a building, might maintain a spreadsheet for this schedule, linked to the actual construction drawings. If someone made a change to these drawings that affected the door schedule, the change would automatically percolate through to the appropriate spreadsheet. Your author has it on authority that this sort of thing has been a fond desire of CAD-using architects for a long time.

We could give you any number of examples where inter-application communications can be true life-savers, even if it's merely a case of being able to view the contents of a database document for which you don't possess a copy of the application with which it was created. The real point is that you can do many of these things using Visual Basic tools. Accessing a database document from within a Visual Basic application is really very easy, for example. You can also use the OLE (Object Linking and Embedding) container control to bring objects from other applications—an Excel spreadsheet, for example—into your Visual Basic applications.

## The Database Control

The Database control lets you establish a link to a database file created by Microsoft Access, FoxPro, dBASE, Paradox, Btrieve, or any database program that supports their file formats. You display information from records in the database through bound controls—text boxes, labels, and picture boxes, for example—which are bound to the Database control and set to display a specified database field. The control itself lets you move around in the database to examine individual records. Figure 18.1 shows an example of the Database control in use on a form.

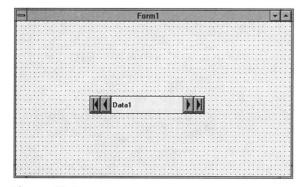

**Figure 18.1**
The Database control.

## Object Linking and Embedding

Object Linking and Embedding—referred to as "OLE" from now on—lets you access and manipulate objects from other applications. These objects can include entire spreadsheets, or individual rows, columns, or cells; paragraphs, lines, or selections from a document; and so on. Using these objects and Visual Basic, you can create a so-called "front-end" application that lets users work with data from one or more different applications, much in the manner of the final report document we talked about at the beginning of this lesson.

The OLE container control is a custom control. Thus, before you can use the OLE container control, you must install its file in your Visual Basic project.

**III**

**Advanced Topics**

The file is called MSOLE2.VBX. See Lesson 13, "Additional User Input," for more information on installing custom controls like MSOLE2.VBX. Once it's installed, you use the OLE container control to access application objects from within Visual Basic applications. Figure 18.2 shows a form with several OLE container controls on it, set to show different data.

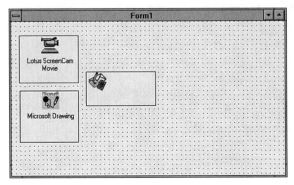

**Figure 18.2**
Three OLE container controls, set to show different data.

In this lesson, we'll concentrate on Visual Basic front-end applications for viewing other applications' data. First we'll look at how to create a front-end application for viewing a specified database document.

# Working with the Database Control

There are just a few steps to using the Database control to create a link to an outside database. These steps are:

1. Draw out a Data control on the appropriate form.

2. Set the DatabaseName and RecordSource properties on the Data control to the database you want to view.

3. Draw controls on the form to display database information. Bind each control to the Data control by putting the Data control's name into the DataSource property.

4. For each display control you've drawn, set the DataField property of the control to display the field within the database that you want to show.

A couple of these steps are worth looking into a little more closely; we'll do so now.

## Linking to an Outside Database

After you've drawn a Data control on your form, the first thing to do is link it to an outside database document. This can be as easy as filling in a database name to the DatabaseName property of the Data control, presuming you're linking to a Microsoft Access database. If not, you must specify with the Connect property of the Data control the type of database to use. The following table shows the appropriate settings.

| *Connect* Property Setting | Corresponding Database Format |
| --- | --- |
| (Leave this Setting Blank) | Microsoft Access |
| foxpro 2.0; | FoxPro Version 2.0 |
| foxpro 2.5; | FoxPro Version 2.5 |
| dbaseIII; | dBASE III |
| dbaseIV; | dBASE IV |
| paradox; pwd=password | Paradox |
| btrieve; | Btrieve |

The semicolon is required after the database name in the Connect property setting.

Another important property to set is the RecordSource property. This property sets a table containing selected field names from the database. If you connect to a database at program design time, a list of available tables appears in the drop-down list for the RecordSource property.

If you want, you can have your program set any of these properties at run time. You'll need to use the Refresh method on the Data control to actually open the specified database once these properties have been set.

## Creating and Binding Control Objects

Before you can view or modify records from a database, you must create areas in which the record's fields can be shown. You do this using controls from the Visual Basic toolbox. The controls you use depend on the kind of data you want to display. To display text data, and allow the user to edit it, you'd use text boxes.

After you create controls for the various fields you want to display from each database record, you must bind each control to the Data control. You do this by entering the name of the Data control (the default name for the first Data control is Data1) into the DataSource property for each control.

The last thing to do is to set which field to display in the control. This is set with the control's DataField property. If you set this property at design time and have already set which database and database table to use, the available fields appear in the drop-down list at the top of the Properties window (see fig. 18.3).

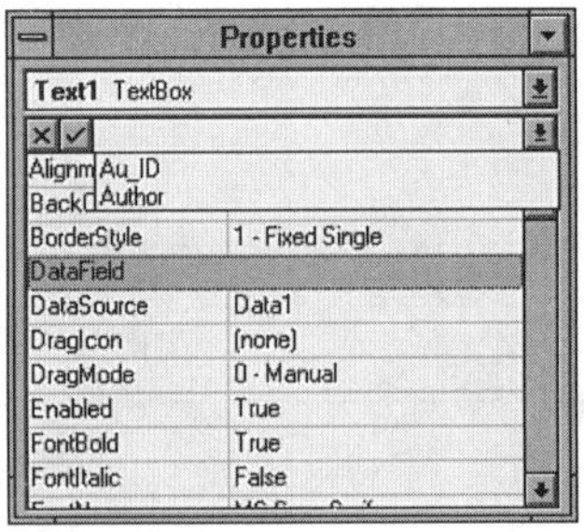

**Figure 18.3**
Choosing a field to display in a bound control.

Note that, as with the name of the database and the name of the database table, you can supply field names to display at run time.

## Manipulating Database Records

At run time, the user clicks one of the four buttons on the Data control to move among records in the database. These controls are shown in Figure 18.4. The leftmost button moves to the first record, the second moves back one record, the third moves forward one record, and the rightmost moves to the last record. Note that you could set the caption on the control to show the name of the database being browsed.

Moves to the first record      Moves forward one record

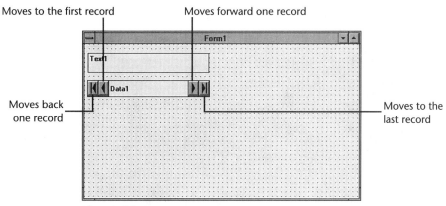

Moves back one record

Moves to the last record

**Figure 18.4**
These buttons on a Data control are used to move among records in the database.

These buttons are functional "right out of the box," as it were; you don't have to write any code to enable the program user to move among records.

You can do more than just look at records, however. If you use text boxes to display text fields from a database, you can allow the user to save any modifications made in these boxes back to the original database. You can also let the user add and delete records. Visual Basic provides three methods that work on the Data control's RecordSet property to provide this functionality. These methods are shown in the following table.

| Method | Effect |
|---|---|
| AddNew | Adds a new record to the database recordset. The contents of all bound controls are immediately cleared to show this new record is blank |
| Update | Saves any changes back out to the database recordset. While you could invoke this method to save changes, note that all changes are saved immediately and automatically if the user clicks a button on the Data control to move to another record |
| Delete | Removes the current record from the database recordset |

Figure 18.5 shows programming code for two command buttons—Add and Delete—intended to give this functionality to a Data control.

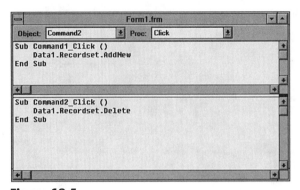

**Figure 18.5**
Letting the user add and delete records so that changes impact the original database.

# Working with the OLE Control

Using the OLE container control is not, in principle, much more difficult than working with the Database control. One way to use the control is to set the object to display and define its data at run time. This is useful for creating front-end applications to new files. The steps involved are as follows:

1. Click the OLE control icon on the toolbox and drag out a control on the appropriate form.

   The Insert Object dialog box appears as shown in Figure 18.6.

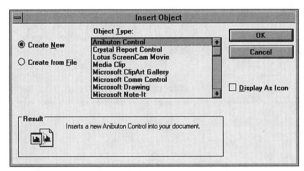

**Figure 18.6**
Choosing the type of OLE object to insert in the control.

2. Choose the object type from among those listed and click OK.

   The appropriate application is started.

3. Enter data for the control in the relevant application.

4. Quit the application to return to Visual Basic.

   Data appears in the control in the same form in which it was entered in the creating application.

## Linked versus Embedded Objects

Before you use the OLE control, you need to understand a crucial difference between linked and embedded objects:

*Linked Objects*        The data for the object is actually maintained in the application that created it, not in the Visual Basic application. This makes the data available to other users and other applications.

*Embedded Objects*   The data for the object is maintained within the Visual Basic application. Other programs can't access it.

## Creating OLE Objects

The method you use to create an OLE object depends, of course, on whether you want the object to be linked or embedded. We outline procedures here for doing both.

To create a *linked* OLE object with an existing file, follow these steps:

1. Drag out an OLE control on the appropriate form.

   The Insert Object dialog box appears.

2. Click the Create from File option button.

3. Click to select the type of object to create.

4. Click the Browse button to display the Browse dialog box.

5. Find the file that you want to link to. Click OK.

6. Click the Link checkbox on the Insert Object dialog box.

7. Click OK to establish the link.

**III**

**Advanced Topics**

To create an *embedded* OLE object with an existing file, follow these steps:

1. Drag out an OLE control on the appropriate form.

   The Insert Object dialog box appears.

2. Click the Create from File option button.

3. Click to select the type of object to create.

4. Click the Browse button to display the Browse dialog box.

5. Find the file that you want to link to. Click OK.

6. Click OK to create the embedded object.

## Getting OLE Data Back into a File

If you want the user to be able to modify embedded data, you have to provide program code that writes these changes back out to the appropriate file. You do this using the appropriate version of the Open and Close commands for the file along with the Action method of the OLE control. Setting the Action equal to 11 saves the file specified by the OLE FileNumber property. Figure 18.7 shows code to save data from an OLE control.

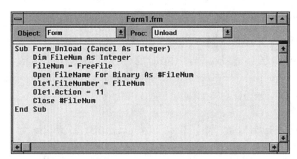

**Figure 18.7**
Saving data from an OLE control to a file.

# Review

In this lesson, you learned the following:

☐ Using inter-application communications, it's possible to pull data from other programs into a Visual Basic project.

☐ You use the Data control to link to existing database documents. This control, when bound to other controls that display data, enables the user to view the contents of a database record by record, and even make changes to this data.

☐ The OLE control lets you link or embed an object from another application into a Visual Basic application. A linked object maintains data in the original application; an embedded object maintains data within the Visual Basic application.

Now you should be ready for the quiz.

# Simplifying Application Creation

## Overview

By now we hope you agree that Visual Basic offers a great many tools and capabilities that can make application programming relatively easy. We haven't quite gotten to the end of these capabilities yet. What's more, there are things you can do yourself as a clever and organized programmer to make future programming projects run more simply and smoothly. By taking advantage of every facet of the Visual Basic package and structuring your projects so that you build on past work, you can leverage your time to maximum effect.

This lesson examines ways to make application creation easier. Topics covered include:

☐ How to write programming code that can be used in other programs

☐ Taking advantage of Help examples and programming code associated with them

☐ Maintaining a library of objects and procedures

☐ Using SetupWizard to create application packages that you can distribute

# Not Reinventing the Wheel

A very great principle of computing is that once a problem has been solved, it should remain solved. That is, if you've discovered some way to program a solution to a problem—creating an amortization schedule for a mortgage, for example—you should be able to re-use that solution in other contexts. This also applies to solutions created by other programmers. Why struggle again to find a solution that someone else has already achieved?

To re-use a computer solution—whether it's a procedure, an entire code module, or even a form—requires that the item in question have been made as general as possible when it was first done. That way, it can be adapted to new contexts and made to work in new programs with minimal changes. It can also be expected to work as advertised.

There are two facets to this problem, as there have been to many problems in this Tutor. First, you can implement programming practices of your own to enable you to re-use your work in later programs. Second, you can take advantage of work that has already been done by other programmers, in particular by those at Microsoft. Let's consider both situations.

## Building on Existing Work

To repeat, building on existing work requires that that work have been made as general as possible. So what does that mean, exactly? We've drawn up a list of a few hints and principles to illustrate.

Ways to build on past work:

☐ Isolate as many activities as possible within individual procedures. No procedure should attempt to accomplish more than one specific task.

☐ Use variables and named constants wherever possible. Using names for constants, rather than entering the values directly, allows different values to be substituted later to adapt the procedure to different circumstances.

☐ Document your programming code so that you can more easily interpret it later, when trying to re-use it. If you enter a single apostrophe (') on a line of code, everything following it is treated by Visual Basic as a comment and doesn't affect program execution.

☐ Look through the examples provided in the Microsoft online help for hints on how to write specific procedures. You can copy Microsoft's example procedures into Visual Basic and then modify them to suit your own purposes.

☐ Find a place on your disk in which to maintain a centralized library of useful procedures and objects. Don't make changes to these objects once they've been archived; rather, copy them as needed and make changes to the copies within new projects.

Figure 19.1 shows two procedures; one is rather specific to a particular case and would be difficult to re-use. The second has been written in a more general form.

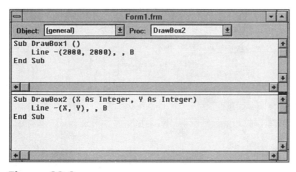

**Figure 19.1**
Two procedures that do the same thing; the second is more generalized.

## Simplified Application Creation

Back in Lesson 3, "Creating a Visual Basic Application," we considered a few steps involved in creating an executable version of a Visual Basic application. While it's true that you could continue to rely on variants of this procedure to make copies of your work to distribute to others, you might not want to. Why not? As it turns out, a Visual Basic application is not entirely self-contained.

Depending on the type and number of custom tools you used to create an application, among other things, a Visual Basic application can actually require more than a dozen separate files to be able to run on someone else's computer system. You can't count on a user having all these files in the correct location, particularly if that user doesn't own a copy of Visual Basic.

If you did get all the necessary files onto a disk (perhaps having had to compress them to save room), you'd present your potential user with the rather daunting task of copying them all to the correct locations on the hard disk. Compressed files then have to be uncompressed. You may know from personal experience that complicated program installation is something users do not appreciate.

Microsoft knows this, too. If you've installed one of their programs (and you have if you installed Visual Basic), then you've encountered their solution to this problem. All Microsoft Windows applications feature a single executable file called SETUP.EXE that you run to install the program. SETUP copies and decompresses all the required files for you.

How do you create such a SETUP file for your own work? Not to be stingy, Microsoft has shared their knowledge of making SETUP files in a nifty application named SetupWizard. This application very nearly automates the process of creating distribution disks for a Visual Basic application. Figure 19.2 shows Visual Basic's SetupWizard at work.

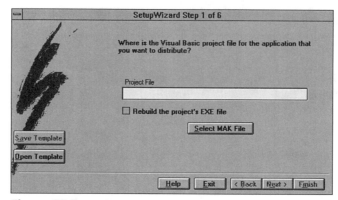

**Figure 19.2**
Using Application SetupWizard for Visual Basic.

As anxious as you undoubtedly are to begin adapting these labor-saving notions to your own work, we'll begin right away with some examples of re-using program code.

# Re-Using Working Program Code

Again, there are two kinds of program items you can re-use: your own and someone else's. There are also a couple of ways in which you can bring such items into a new project. You can copy them to the Clipboard and then use the Paste command. In some cases, though, you can use the Add File and Load Text commands in the File menu to bring predefined items directly into a project.

## About the Sample Applications and Help Examples

Other people's work is the easiest place for us to begin. Microsoft has included two types of re-usable entities directly with Visual Basic. One set resides in the online help. Almost every object, procedure, and function documented in the help includes an example of how to program for it. Figure 19.3 shows such a code example in the Help window.

```
                          Visual Basic Help                     
 Open Statement Example                        Close   Copy   Print

 This example uses Open to open a file for output. To try this example, paste the code into the
 Declarations section of a form. Then press F5 and click the form.

 Sub Form_Click ()
     Dim FName, FNum, I, Msg, TestString      ' Declare variables.
     TestString = "The quick brown fox"        ' Create test string.
     For I = 1 To 5
         FNum = FreeFile                        ' Determine file number.
         FName = "TEST" & FNum & ".DAT"
         Open FName For Output As FNum          ' Open file.
         Print #I, TestString                   ' Write string to file.
     Next I
     Close                                      ' Close all files.
     Msg = "Several test files have been created on your disk. "
     Msg = Msg & "Choose OK to remove the test files."
     MsgBox Msg
     Kill "TEST?.DAT"                           ' Remove test files.
 End Sub
```

**Figure 19.3**
A programming code example in the online help.

Follow these steps to copy a help example into an open Visual Basic project:

1. Use the Help menu's Contents or Search commands to open a Help window, locating an item for which you want to copy a code example.

2. Click the heading Example at the top of the window.

   The code example appears.

3. Click the Copy button on the Example window.

   A dialog box appears like that shown in Figure 19.4.

III

Advanced Topics

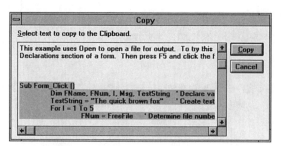

**Figure 19.4**
Choosing what to copy from an example.

4. Click and drag to select the portion of the example to copy.

5. Click the Copy button.

    The dialog box closes and the selected text is copied to the Clipboard.

6. Close the Help window and return to the form that you want to paste the code example into. Double-click the form to open the Code window.

7. Choose Paste from the Edit menu to place the copied example into the Code window. Make changes as desired.

Microsoft has also included a number of sample programs in the Visual Basic package. They use these sample programs throughout their own program documentation to illustrate important points and to show you how key features may be used. You can copy anything out of these samples to adapt to your own projects. Figure 19.5 shows one of the sample applications loaded into Visual Basic.

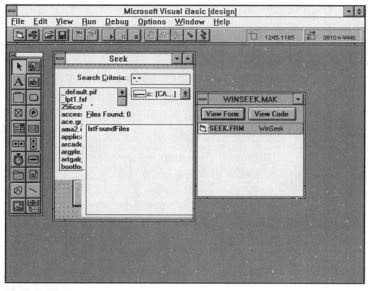

**Figure 19.5**
The WINSEEK.MAK example program.

Sample projects from Microsoft include:

| Project Name | Function |
| --- | --- |
| ALARM.MAK | An application that illustrates use of the timer control. It's found in \VB\SAMPLES\ENVIR |
| BIBLIO.MAK | Shows how to use the data control. Located in \VB\SAMPLES\BIBLIO |
| BLANKER.MAK | A screen saver; illustrates use of graphics methods and controls. Found in \VB\SAMPLES\GRAPHICS |
| OLE2DEMO.MAK | Shows how to use object linking and embedding. This project is located in \VB\SAMPLES\OLE2 |
| RECEDIT.MAK | An application to edit database records. Shows file processing concepts. Look for it in \VB\SAMPLES\FILEIO |
| TEXTEDIT.MAK | Also illustrates file system management, in a small text editor. Found in \VB\SAMPLES\MENUS |
| WINSEEK.MAK | Illustrates use of the File System controls in an application to find files. Located in \VB\SAMPLES\FILECTLS |

**III**

**Advanced Topics**

There are several other sample applications available. Browse through the SAMPLES subdirectory to see them.

Many of these sample projects contain forms or sections of code that you might want to use. To maintain the original files to use again elsewhere, you should create a copy of any part of an existing project you want to use for your own work. Use the Add File command to add the copy to your current project.

To add a file (form or code module) from a sample application to a project of your own, follow these steps:

1. Use the Windows File Manager to make a copy of the file you want to use. (Remember that forms have the .FRM extension and code modules have an extension of .BAS.) Move this copy to the working directory of your current project.

2. Within Visual Basic, choose the Add File command from the File menu.

   The Add File dialog box appears (see fig. 19.6).

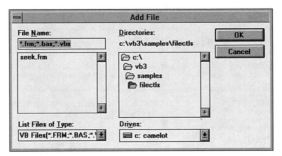

**Figure 19.6**
The Add File dialog box.

3. Locate the new file's name and click to select it. Click OK.

   The file is added to the current project and the dialog box goes away.

## Creating Your Own Code Library

Just as Visual Basic has a library of example applications in the SAMPLES directory, you can create and maintain your own library of forms and procedures. Keeping a centralized location is more certain than simply trying to copy elements from your existing applications; if you ever delete one of these applications that had outlived its usefulness, the code you developed in it is also lost. Often, procedures can outlive the applications containing them. Maintaining a library can help you make sure useful procedures live on. Figure 19.7 shows what such a code library might look like from within the Windows File Manager.

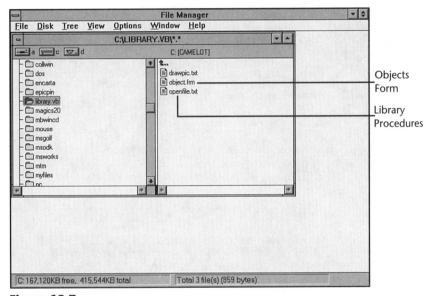

**Figure 19.7**
A Visual Basic code library, which consists of three files within a directory called LIBRARY.VB.

When managing a library of your own, think about these points:

☐ Create a separate directory for your library. You might give it a name like LIBRARY.VB.

☐ Visual Basic lets you save segments of code as text, which you can later bring directly into another project. Use the Save Text and Load Text commands in the File Menu to do this. This lets you save individual procedures if you like.

☐ You might consider maintaining one or more forms whose sole purpose is to store useful objects and their procedures. Copy an object to the Clipboard and then paste it into your library form. (OBJECTS.FRM might be a good name for it.) You'll have to copy its associated procedures separately using the Clipboard as well. Later, you can copy any of these objects to the Clipboard and then paste them into a project.

☐ Include liberal comments with each segment of code, so that you'll later be able to remember what it does. Type an apostrophe at the end of a line of code before typing a comment. Explain what each segment of code does and expects.

Follow these steps to save a section of code from an application in text format:

1. With the appropriate project open, click a form to open the Code window.

2. Locate the procedure you want to save.

3. Choose the Save Text command from the File menu.

   The Save Text dialog box appears (see fig. 19.8).

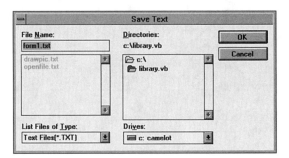

**Figure 19.8**
The Save Text dialog box.

4. Give the code segment a name (end with the extension .TXT). Be sure to use the directory list to switch into your code library directory before saving. Click OK to save the segment.

5. Use the Load Text command to bring an existing, saved text segment into a new Visual Basic project.

Follow this procedure to create a master form on which to store objects from other projects for future use:

1. Within a project containing one or more objects you want to save, click the Add Form button on the toolbar to add a new form; this will be the library form.

2. With the new form active, choose the Save File command in the File menu. Give the library form a name like OBJECTS.FRM.

3. Use the Copy command to copy selected controls to the Clipboard. Paste the copies onto the Objects form.

4. You must copy the programming code associated with each object separately. Use the Copy command to copy procedures from the Code window for the original form to the Code window for the Objects form.

5. When all desired objects from the current project have been copied, choose Save File with the Objects form active to save it. Then choose Remove File from the File menu to release the Objects form from the project.

6. Choose the Open Project command from the File menu to open another project with objects you want to save.

7. Choose the Add File command to temporarily bring the Objects form into this project.

8. Copy objects onto the Objects form as described in Step 3. Save the form and then remove it from this project as in Step 4.

9. Repeat Steps 5–8 for each project containing controls you want to save.

Figure 19.9 shows an objects form with useful objects from different projects. It's a simple procedure to temporarily add this form to a new project, copy objects from it, and then release the form using the Remove File command.

III

**Advanced Topics**

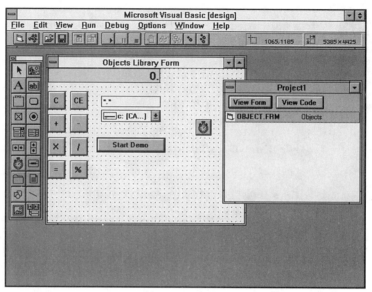

**Figure 19.9**
An objects library form can hold many useful objects for you to re-use in future
projects.

**Caution** Be careful how you name objects and procedures. The more specific your names, the
better, especially when you're creating an objects form. You'll have trouble copying items
that have the same name. Make sure your objects form itself has a name other than
Form1, Form2, or the like. Otherwise, Visual Basic may not let you bring it into a new
project to copy from it.

## Creating an Executable Application

Now, we turn to our last topic in how to take advantage of existing work.
Presuming you've got a valuable application you want to distribute, you can
use SetupWizard, which is included with the Visual Basic package, to make
distribution disks for your program.

Follow these steps to use SetupWizard to create a distributable version of your application:

1. Double-click its icon to run SetupWizard.

2. Enter the pathname (disk, directory, and file name) of the project file for which you want to create a distribution disk.

   Remember that the project file has an extension .MAK. Click Next to continue.

3. Select any special features supported by your application. Click Next.

4. Choose the disk drive to use and the type of disks to support. Click Next.

5. Add or remove files from the list shown as needed. Click Next.

6. Follow screen prompts to create the distribution disks.

# Review

In this lesson, you learned the following:

☐ Writing generalized programming code leaves more opportunity for you to re-use that code in other contexts.

☐ The examples in the online help contain sections of code that you can copy onto the Clipboard, paste into your own projects, and edit as needed.

☐ Visual Basic comes with a number of sample applications from which you might want to copy forms, objects, and procedures.

III

Advanced Topics

☐ You can create your own code library of useful procedures and objects. Procedures can be stored in text format, and brought back into a project later. You can store objects you intend to re-use on a special objects form and then, as needed, bring this form into new projects and copy objects from it.

☐ Visual Basic's SetupWizard takes you step-by-step through the process of creating application packages that you can distribute.

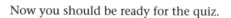

**Quiz**

Now you should be ready for the quiz.

# PLUG YOURSELF INTO...

# THE MACMILLAN INFORMATION SUPERLIBRARY™

## Free information and vast computer resources from the world's leading computer book publisher—online!

### FIND THE BOOKS THAT ARE RIGHT FOR YOU!

A complete online catalog, plus sample chapters and tables of contents give you an in-depth look at *all* of our books, including hard-to-find titles. It's the best way to find the books you need!

- **STAY INFORMED** with the latest computer industry news through our online newsletter, press releases, and customized Information SuperLibrary Reports.

- **GET FAST ANSWERS** to your questions about MCP books and software.

- **VISIT** our online bookstore for the latest information and editions!

- **COMMUNICATE** with our expert authors through e-mail and conferences.

- **DOWNLOAD SOFTWARE** from the immense MCP library:
    - Source code and files from MCP books
    - The best shareware, freeware, and demos

- **DISCOVER HOT SPOTS** on other parts of the Internet.

- **WIN BOOKS** in ongoing contests and giveaways!

**TO PLUG INTO MCP:** →

GOPHER: gopher.mcp.com
FTP: ftp.mcp.com

**WORLD WIDE WEB: http://www.mcp.com**

# Notes

# Notes

# Notes

# Notes

# Notes

# Notes

# Notes

# Notes

# Notes

# Notes

# Notes

# Notes

# Notes

# Licensing Agreement

By opening this package, you are agreeing to be bound by the following agreement:

This software product is copyrighted, and all rights are reserved by the publisher and author. You are licensed to use this software on a single computer. You may copy and/or modify the software as needed to facilitate your use of it on a single computer. Making copies of the software for any other purpose is a violation of the United States copyright laws.

This software is sold *as is* without warranty of any kind, either expressed or implied, including but not limited to the implied warranties of merchantability and fitness for a particular purpose. Neither the publisher nor its dealers or distributors assume any liability for any alleged or actual damages arising from the use of this program. (Some states do not allow for the exclusion of implied warranties, so the exclusion may not apply to you.)